# The Savannah Monitor Lizard
## The Truth about *Varanus exanthematicus*

Daniel Bennett & Ravi Thakoordyal

# Viper Press
GLOSSOP, ENGLAND

# The Savannah Monitor Lizard
## The Truth about *Varanus exanthematicus*

© Daniel Bennett and Ravi Thakoordyal 2003

ISBN: 0-9526632-9-5

Printed in the United States of America

Published by
**Viper Press**
118 Sheffield Road
Glossop
SK13 8QU
England


www.mampam.com

# Contents

# Acknowledgements

Much of the husbandry information included in this book was pioneered by Frank Retes of Goanna Ranch, Tucson, Arizona. We are very grateful to him for sharing his expertise, although we in no way imply that he agrees with the statements in this book. We are also grateful to the people who made helpful comments on portions of the manuscript, although again we do not imply that they agree with our opinions. Katie Hampson did most of the typesetting of the book, designed the cover and made many useful comments on the text and layout. Finally, this book might never have become a reality were it not for the support of Sylvia and Les Hampson.
**Daniel Bennett & Ravi Thakoordyal.**

I am particularly grateful to Bature Ali of Accra, whose good humour, great skill and tenacity have been invaluable throughout my work on wild savannah monitors. Ghana Wildlife Department has been very supportive of the work. Thanks especially to to G.A. Punguse, B.Y. Ofori Frimpong, N.K. Ankudey, B. Basuglo and Lou. Additional fieldworkers were Wahab Belu, Awdu, Seidu and Momii Yedu, Wilson Akonnor, Sulemana Adamu, Jake Paul, Polly Crouch, members of the Kyabobo Conservation Project, Aberdeen University Black Volta Project and Tunbridge Wells Girls' Grammar School. At Aberdeen University Dr M. Swaine (Department of Plant and Soil Science) provided many of the initial contacts that made this work possible.
**Daniel Bennett**, Phnom Pehn, March 2002.

I would especially like to express my gratitude to Debbie Anderson and Rakesh Thakoordyal for their continued support and encouragement in this hobby. As well I would like to say a word of thanks to the monitor keeping community as a whole for their direct and indirect education on varanid husbandry. We all know that monitor keeping is a continuing education that can be made easier as long as we continue to share our experiences and listen to our monitors.
**Ravi Thakoordyal**, Toronto, April 2002.

## *Additional Illustrations*

Thanks to Dale Harmon, Nicky Green, Natural History Museum London, Jan Wieringa, Daniel Tupper/Portsmouth Reptile and Amphibian Association, Pier Luigi Vianello, Alfred Ojeda, Christine Himes and Dieter Mahsberg for providing illustrations or access to animals. All other illustrations by Daniel Bennett or Ravi Thakoordyal.

## *Why another book on savannah monitors?*

In the 1990s over a quarter of a million live savannah monitors were exported from West Africa to supply demand from pet keepers in North America and Europe. But despite the great interest in this animal, there is very little reliable information available about its biology and behaviour. Reports of captive breeding are extremely rare and details of their requirements in captivity are lacking in the literature. The books we have seen that are devoted to "savannah monitors" are unsatisfactory, at least partly because they confuse them with the much larger white-throated monitor that lives in southern Africa, but also because the authors have neither benefited from seeing the animal in its natural environment nor had any experience of breeding the animals in captivity. Kept in the manner suggested by other books the lizards will, at best, survive, but they will not flourish. Without a good understanding of how the lizards behave in nature and how they should be kept in captivity, the vast majority will die long, lingering deaths at the hands of well meaning, but misinformed keepers. We hope this book will provide some reliable information on this remarkable and much maligned reptile, and give its fans some indication of its proper care in captivity. It is by no means the last word on the savannah monitor (it has barely scratched the surface) but it will hopefully bridge the gap between the many well-meaning but misinformed books and magazine articles on keeping these lizards in captivity and the largely inaccessible facts about how the animal spends its natural life and how it can thrive in captivity.

## *What is a monitor lizard?*

Monitor lizards are a family of reptiles (Varanidae) that includes the mighty Komodo dragon and at least 50 other species found in many habitats throughout Africa, southern Asia and Australia. They are easily recognised by their long, forked tongues and the presence of small scales on the head. Although some species are giant lizards many dwarf species also exist. All but two species are entirely carnivorous and they swallow their prey whole. Because of their size they are of considerable economic importance in some of the poorest countries in the world. Monitor lizards do not look very inconspicuous, but new species (many growing over 150cm (5 feet) long) are still being discovered every year!

## *What is a savannah monitor?*

Savannah monitor lizards are *Varanus exanthematicus*, also known as Bosc's monitor lizard after the French scientist Louis Bosc who first described the species in 1792[15]. The savannah monitor is entirely distinct from the white-throated monitor *Varanus albigularis*, although the two species have been regularly confused with each other for the last 200 years. One of the reasons we wrote this book was that other guides to savannah monitors constantly confuse the two species, giving the reader completely incorrect information. In fact virtually everything written in other books about savannah monitors is actually based on white-throated monitors.

Savannah monitors are most easily recognised by the large flat scales over the neck. In contrast the white-throated monitor has much smaller scales. Both species vary greatly in pattern, but savannah monitors usually have indistinctly banded tails, a ground colour of dull grey, brown or olive green and some lighter spots over the back.

Savannah monitors belong to a group within the monitor family known as *Polydaedalus*[27], together with the white-throated monitor *V. albigularis*, the Nile monitor *V. niloticus*, the ornate forest monitor *V. ornatus*, the Yemen monitor *V. yemenensis* and the extinct *V. rusingiensis*[21] from Lake Victoria. All members of the group show adaptations that enable them to crush strong shells and it is likely that all can survive on a diet composed only of molluscs when the need arises.

The following pages contain a key to the monitor lizards of Africa that can be used to identify the various species. Starting at the top decide which of the two statements is most relevant and work through the key accordingly.

## Key to African monitor lizards

1. Tail round in cross section, without a pronounced dorsal ridge............................................*Varanus griseus*
Tail at least partly compressed in cross section with a double ridge......................................................2

2. Less than 100 scales around midbody. Neck with large, flat, oval scales, nostril equidistant between eye and tip of snout. Usually less than 120cm total length. Body colour brown.............................*Varanus exanthematicus*
More than 100 scales at midbody. Neck scales either not enlarged or slightly enlarged with keel.................3

3. Tail strongly compressed in cross section. Body colour green/black........................................................4
Tail only slightly compressed, nostril closer to eye than tip of snout. Body colour brown......*Varanus albigularis*

4. Tongue pink, up to five rows of light coloured spots on the back.........................................*Varanus ornatus*
Tongue dark. More than five rows of spots on the back...........................................*Varanus niloticus*

**Figure 1. Savannah Monitor from Abokobi, Ghana.**

7

Figure 2. The savannah monitor *Varanus exanthematicus*, note the larger scales and position of the nostril.

Figure 3. White-throated monitor lizard *Varanus albigularis*.

Figure 4. Details of the neck and dorsal scales of *Varanus albigularis* (left) and
*V. exanthematicus* (right). Preserved animals from the Natural History
Museum, London.

## What other monitor lizards live in Africa?

In the Sahara Desert lives the desert monitor, *Varanus griseus* (figure 35), an unusually bad tempered lizard that is also found in Asian deserts east as far as Pakistan and India. The desert monitor is not rare and it is one of the few species whose skin is of no value. Nevertheless international trade in the desert monitor is completely prohibited and so the animals are rarely seen as pets, which is probably for the best considering their uncompromising temperaments.

The Nile monitor *Varanus niloticus* (figure 34) lives throughout Africa, almost wherever there is a permanent supply of water. This is a large lizard known by virtually everybody, including city inhabitants. Baby Nile monitors are often available as pets, but because of their very lively dispositions and the huge sizes they reach, require much more care than most people can provide. An even larger lizard is the ornate monitor, *Varanus ornatus*, a forest dwelling species which probably should be of conservation concern in many West African countries. This species is also sometimes available in the pet trade but is even more demanding than the Nile monitor.

In southern Africa the savannah monitor is replaced by the white-throated and black-throated monitors *V. albigularis albigularis* (Figure 32) and *V. albigularis microstictus*. These monitors grow larger than savannah monitors, have a more varied diet and, although they are much less common in the pet trade, there are a growing number of captive bred individuals available.

Finally there are unconfirmed reports of a very large and presently unknown species of monitor lizard living in the forests of the Congo[14]. Incredibly more species of huge lizards are still being discovered every year, and not many people will be surprised if another species is added to the list.

You can read more about these lizards in our list of recommended publications at the back of this book.

## Why is there confusion over savannah monitors?

Mainly because prior to 1990 the name *Varanus exanthematicus* was shared by the savannah monitor and the white/black-throated monitors *Varanus albigularis albigularis* and *V. albigularis microstictus*. *Varanus albigularis* is a very different animal from the savannah monitor. It grows much larger than the savannah monitor, has a much more varied diet and occurs in many temperate regions of southern Africa. Although it is seen in the pet trade, it is nowhere near as common as the savannah monitor. However there is very little first hand information about the savannah monitor available in print, whereas there is considerable literature on *V. albigularis*, probably because it is a much larger animal and not as secretive as the savannah monitor.

In fact, most people who live in areas inhabited by savannah monitors have never seen them, not because they are rare but because they are extremely secretive animals. Unlike Nile monitors they cannot be attracted to baited traps, so catching them requires either a fortunate encounter or a search for their hiding places. As a result the animal is often mistaken by local people for a "land crocodile"

There is also confusion because although the savannah monitor is an extremely popular pet, very few people have ever succeeded in breeding them and there have been very few investigations into their ecology in the wild. This is unfortunate, because given proper care the savannah monitor can be very prolific, and studying the animal in the wild is a very rewarding experience, not least because it lives in some of the friendliest and most hospitable (and sadly the poorest) countries on Earth.

## Are there different subspecies of savannah monitor?

Maybe. In 1827 a man called Heyden[24] described a lizard from Sudan as Varanus ocellatus, which was subsequently thought to be just an alternative name for either V.exanthematicus or V. albigularis. Rumours that the animals are different from either species have persisted[5,6], but the specimens that I (DB) have examined (including the collection of the Natural History Museum, London (from Anseba, Niora Road and south of Meshra) and many skins exported into Egypt from Sudan) all look like regular savannah monitors to me. It is possible that another, presently unknown, monitor lizard lives in Sudan.

VARANUS OCELLATUS
Anseba Valley, Abyssinia.

**Figure 5. "*Varanus ocellatus*" from Sudan (from Anderson 1898[1])**

## Where do savannah monitors come from?

Savannah monitors are found in sub-Saharan Africa; from Senegal east to Sudan, south almost to the Congo River and the Rift Valley. Savannah monitors in the pet trade are almost exclusively from Ghana, Togo, Benin and Nigeria.

**Figure 6. Approximate distribution of *Varanus exanthematicus***

## What sort of habitats do savannah monitors live in?

As its name implies, the savannah monitor is principally a creature of grasslands. These include vast swathes of high grasses almost completely devoid of trees, open areas with scattered bushes, rocky hillsides and woodlands with grassy undergrowth. Grasslands in West Africa are most simply classified as; **sahel** - dry grasslands with short rainy seasons close to the edge of the Sahara Desert; **Guinea** - more luscious grasslands with many more tree species and a longer growing season; **coastal** grasslands separated from the Guinea zone by the rain-forest belt. The savannah monitor is found in all three zones. The only studied populations occur in the sahel grasslands of Sudan, where the lizards live around seasonal ponds[18] and in the coastal grasslands of Ghana where they are found in farms and bushland devoid of surface water[9]. Savannah monitors have not been found in closed-canopy woodlands where lack of sunshine on the ground

Figure 7. The coastal plain of Ghana, origin of most pet savannah monitors.

Figure 8. Uncultivated habitat at Shai Hills Game Reserve, Ghana.

prevents grasses from growing, nor in very dry bushland on desert fringes. They appear to be entirely absent from rainforest, and as a result the animals in the coastal grasslands along the Gulf of Guinea are apparently isolated from the main population by the rainforest belt. When the rainforest was intact the only apparent route of gene flow was through the Dahomey Gap. Today so little forest remains that there is no real barrier between the grasslands. The little DNA evidence available suggests that the coastal population are typical savannah monitors.

13

The climates in these areas are characterised by a dry season with little or no rainfall and higher temperatures and a wet season which varies in intensity depending on the proximity of the Sahara desert. The animals' behaviour is highly seasonal with most feeding occurring during the rainy season and courtship and mating early in the dry season. Later in the dry season the animals' activity is greatly reduced until favourable conditions return.

## What shelters do savannah monitors use?

The usual shelters of savannah monitors are burrows, abandoned termite mounds and tree hollows. Savannah monitors like to find tight spaces to wedge themselves into, often crevices that seem impossibly small. They use these retreats to spend the nights, hide from predators and ride out dry weather.

The burrows used by savannah monitors are usually excavated by other animals and adapted by the lizards. Juveniles in the coastal plain of Ghana invariably shelter in the burrow of the giant cricket (*Brachytrupes membranaceus)* wherever these are available, otherwise they shelter in the holes of large scorpions, mice or amphibians. As they grow the lizards continually expand the entrance of the burrow, digging both with the claws and by shaving earth from the sides of the burrow with the hard ridges at either side of the head. Monitor burrows are fairly easy to recognise after a bit of practice, because they have a characteristic oval-shaped opening and the area around the burrow entrance is kept scrupulously clean and free from debris. Temperatures in these burrows are relative stable compared with surface temperatures and humidity inside the burrow is considerably higher than outside. One hundred and thirteen burrows examined by me had an average depth of 30cm [12 inches] (range 11-100cm [4-43 inches]). Juveniles never shelter in burrows made by larger animals, nor in abandoned termite mounds, presumably because of the very real likelihood of predators lurking in such shelters.

**Figure 9. Savannah Monitor investigating a burrow.**

Figure 10. *Brachytrupes* burrow occupied by young savannah monitor.

## Do savannah monitors climb trees?

Figure 11. Savannah-rainforest transition habitat at Krachi Nkwanta, Ghana.

The savannah monitor is not a particularly agile climber, but I regularly find them resting on the branches of trees and bushes. They climb trees throughout the year, but perhaps most commonly during very wet weather (when burrows may be flooded) and in very dry conditions when activity is greatly reduced. It seems that they use trees as basking areas, particularly in heavily wooded grasslands. I have never found any evidence that the animals catch food in trees, but in Senegal a lot of prey are taken from bushes and trees, particularly among *Ipomea* flowers[19]. When disturbed in trees they generally jump to the ground, not sustaining injuries even when falling from the top of tall trees.

15

## Do savannah monitors hibernate?

No. Savannah monitors live in tropical places where temperatures never get cold enough to require hibernation. The animals are forced to reduce activity during very dry periods, but they never become torpid and are awake throughout the year. In Senegal this period of inactivity lasts from approximately November to April[18], in Ghana from January to March[9].

## Do savannah monitors thermoregulate?

The places savannah monitors inhabit are dense mosaics of sunlight and shadow that allow the animals access to a wide range of ambient temperatures. This gives them the opportunity to be very precise thermoregulators. Burrows used by savannah monitors maintain fairly constant temperatures which are warmer than surface temperature at night and lower than surface temperatures during the day. This means that the savannah monitors wake up with body temperatures of 25-26°C [77-79°F], which are then kept between 30 and 35°C [86 - 95°F] for most of the day, rising to over 39°C [102°F] for short periods. For much of the year the lizards are at risk from overheating if they spend too long out in the open. This is particularly a problem for juveniles who heat up much faster than adults and can survive only a few minutes under full sun. Gruesome experiments have shown that most monitor lizards die when their body temperatures exceed

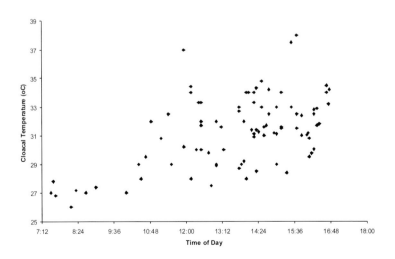

**Figure 12. Graph showing cloacal temperatures of juvenile savannah monitor lizards captured in the coastal plane of Ghana. [25°C=77°F, 39°C=102°F]**

Figure 13. Savannah monitor hunter at work in the coastal plain of Ghana. This abandoned termite mound contained a large savannah monitor and a spitting cobra. It took two hours to excavate!

42°C [106.7°F][2]. A humane version of the same experiment (Figure 14) demon-
strates that on a sunny morning an 11g [0.4 ounce] juvenile increased body
temperature by 1.7°C [3°F] in a minute, whilst a 400g [14 ounce] adult heated at
only 0.2°C [0.4°F] per minute. Furthermore juvenile lizards heat up as if they
were inert objects but adults are able to maintain steady body temperatures of
around 38°C [100°F] for much longer periods. This means that when juveniles
reach their maximum preferred body temperature they must retreat to a cooler
spot within two minutes, whilst adults can remain active in full sun for a further
half an hour. This greatly increases the animals foraging options in hot weather,
but because it takes the lizards much longer to heat up they are unable to make
much use of short sunny spells during cloudy weather. As a result juveniles can
be active on any day when there are breaks in the cloud, but adults must remain
inactive unless more substantial sunny periods are available.

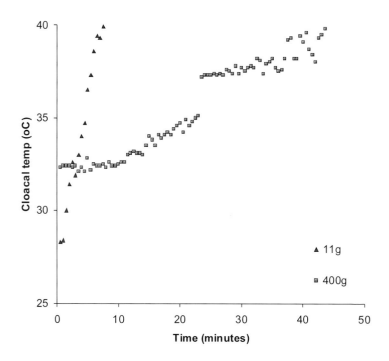

**Figure 14. Heating rates of restrained juvenile and adult savannah monitors.
These animals were released unharmed. [30°C=86°F, 40°C=104°F]**

## Are savannah monitors solitary?

Savannah monitors are usually very shy animals, rarely seen by people except when they are running away. Their habitat makes observing individuals difficult and there has never been a study of the behaviour of adult animals in the wild. As a result very little is known about the social structure of savannah monitor populations. We know that they are not territorial, in the sense that they do not actively protect their activity area from other lizards, but they may well fight each other over access to resources such as food, mates or nesting sites.

Newly-hatched savannah monitors remain close to their nest sites for at least the first nine months of life, and although they are found in dense clusters they seem to avoid each other's burrows. Older animals are often found in close proximity to each other; often in the same tree or bush, more rarely in the same burrow. I (DB) have never found adult males and females sharing the same retreat, but it seems reasonable to expect that this happens, particularly during the breeding season.

Given the high densities of savannah monitors in many areas it is safe to assume that individuals sharing the same activity area are acquainted with each other, but the nature of their interactions and the role they play in determining any social hierarchy remain unknown.

The problem of observing monitor lizards in their day-to-day life is not insurmountable. Recent studies of the desert monitor[32,33,34] have revealed many fascinating facets of monitor lizards' social behaviour that were previously entirely unknown. We know from studies of other species that monitor lizards establish hierarchies by using highly ritualised combat, allowing the lizards to test their strength against each other without the risks that a free-for-all fight would entail. Often this combat takes the form of a bipedal wrestling match in which the combatants stand on their hind legs embracing each other around the chest and attempting to push their opponent over[25]. As far as I am aware this behaviour has not been observed in savannah monitors, although it almost certainly occurs. Adults of many monitor species show characteristic scars over the back, which are presumed to be the result of these contests, but among savannah monitors I have only noticed them on females. There are few published observations on courtship in the savannah monitor, but in other species males scratch the females (especially on the neck and back), tongue them (particularly in areas of the body rich in scent glands) and encourage the female to lift her tail base by scratching at it with the hind claws whilst straddling her. It has been suggested that some monitor lizards form loose pair bonds, which would serve to reduce the risk of injuries sustained during courtship between unacquainted individuals.

## *What do savannah monitors eat?*

The savannah monitor is a habitual digger and spends much of its time sniffing out prey buried below the surface and rooting about in leaf litter. Almost all the prey of savannah monitors are invertebrates and snails. The only vertebrates regularly eaten are amphibians. Mammals are eaten only extremely rarely - just one example has been found in over 1000 samples!

The usual way scientists investigate diet in lizards is to cut animals open and record their gut contents -a reliable method but lacking compassion and

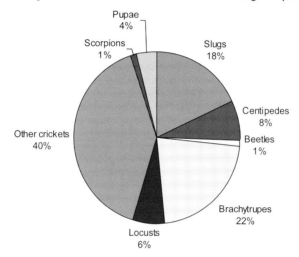

**Figure 15. Diet of 8-week old savannah monitors in the coastal plain of Ghana**

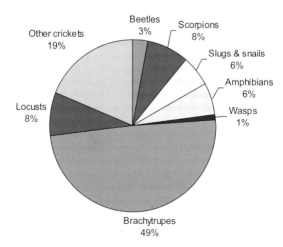

**Figure 16. Diet of 5-6 month old savannah monitors in the coastal plain of Ghana**

precluding the possibility of the animal eating anything else. In the search for less drastic techniques I have taken faeces and stomach flushings from hundreds of savannah monitors caught and released in the coastal plain of Ghana. Neither gives a true indication of the diet (for example faeces miss amphibians, stomach flushings miss snails) but used together they give a fair representation[7,9].

The diet of savannah monitors depends on the size of the lizards and the foods it has access to. The most detailed studies of diet have been conducted in areas of Ghana where the animals are often caught for export. Here newly hatched lizards feed mainly on small crickets, locusts and slugs. Within a few weeks they are also feeding on snails, smaller scorpions, the giant cricket *Brachytrupes membranaceus* and the pedipalps of large emperor scorpions (*Pandinus*). Within months they are large enough to swallow emperor scorpions whole, and these along with *Brachytrupes* continue to be the main foods for the first year of life. The giant cricket is so important in the lives of young savannah monitors that I have given it its own section in this book (page 42). Larger savannah monitors rarely feed on *Brachytrupes*, perhaps because they are too large to enter their burrows and would have to spend an hour or more digging them out. The prey eaten by young savannah monitors are much larger than those taken by juvenile Nile and Bengal monitors[4,11]. Young savannah monitors often consume prey items a third of their own body weight. The usual foods of adults in Ghana are giant millipedes (*Iulus* species), snails, scorpions, larval and adult beetles, crickets and locusts, most of which are found on or beneath the ground. In Senegal adults find most of their food in bushes and beneath ruminant dung[19]. There the diet is also composed largely of giant millipedes, beetles and their larvae, with a shift towards crickets later in the wet season.

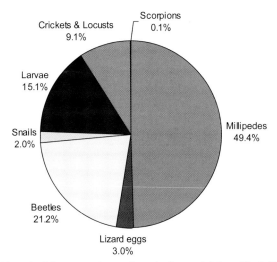

**Figure 17. Diet of adult savannah monitors in Senegal (after Cissé 1972)**

21

**Figure 18. Black scorpion (*Pandinus imperator*), a favourite food of the savannah monitor. Picture courtesy of Dieter Mahsberg.**

All *Polydaedalus* monitor lizards (see page 6) are adept at cracking snail shells with their very powerful jaws and robust teeth. As the animals grow older the jaw bones thicken, the associated muscles get more massive and the tooth shape changes to become blunt and peglike, allowing the lizards to exert a massive amount of pressure in their bite. The only other monitor lizards that show these adaptations live in the Philippines Islands, where they feed almost exclusively on fruit, snails and crab legs[2,10]. It is interesting that molluscivory is so important to all monitor lizards in sub Saharan Africa, whilst in Asia and Australia it is a very unusual strategy.

**Figure 19. Gray's monitor lizard *Varanus olivaceus,* has dentition similar to that of the savannah monitor for crushing snails.**

## *What eats Savannah monitors?*

Important predators of savannah monitors are birds, other monitors, snakes, cats of all sizes and people. Although no hard data exists, I think the most important predators of savannah monitors are probably birds, especially hawks that constantly cruise over the grasslands.

The best known predators of savannah monitors are snakes; spitting cobras, garter snakes and pythons are all known to feed on the lizards[9,12,26]. Of these the cobra is perhaps the most significant. They use many of the same shelters that adults favour, especially abandoned termite mounds, and old rodent or squirrel burrows, and the fact that these snakes are very likely to be encountered in burrows that are inhabited by small mammals may be an important reason why savannah monitors very rarely eat rodents. Some monitor lizards have been shown to be immune to the venom of vipers and cobras[29], but no experiments on the effect of these toxins on savannah monitors have been performed.

Snakes almost always catch savannah monitors by entering their burrows, usually at night. Unless the lizard can hide its shelter there is little it can do to defend itself. A possible option is to block the snake's route with its tailbase, but only the biggest males are large enough to fill the burrow lumen. Other monitors have burrows with an escape shaft dug just below the surface, which the lizards can break through to freedom if cornered. No such escape plan features in the defence strategy of the savannah monitor, but it does appear to have evolved at least two behaviours that give it some chance against a hungry snake. The first of these was first recorded in 1919 from a lizard caught in the northern Congo[30] which became completely lifeless, grasping one of its hind feet firmly in its mouth.

**Figure 20. Defensive posture of savannah monitor from Schmidt 1919.**

In 1994 one lizard in a bag of 22 young savannah monitors I was examining had exactly the same posture. It remained like that for 24 hours but in my ignorance, I presumed it had been hit on the head whilst being dug from its burrow. In hindsight this behaviour has most likely evolved to make the lizard difficult to swallow. It is interesting that the behaviour is so rarely observed, perhaps suggesting only a small proportion of animals inherit it, or that very specific stimuli are required to trigger the reaction. I have observed a more common defence against snakes when inexperienced hunters put a savannah monitor into the same bag as a python. The lizard seizes the snake around the neck in a bulldog-like grip and holds on indefinitely. People collecting animals for the pet trade are well aware of this reaction, which eventually results in the suffocation of the snake. They report that it is impossible to get the lizard to release its grip without injuring it.

## How do savannah monitors spend their time?

Savannah monitors spend a lot of their time just resting, in burrows or on bushes and branches. When they are not resting they are usually digging. In bad weather or when prey is scarce the lizards remain in their retreats, sometimes for weeks or months at a time. They use little energy during these times and loose weight very slowly. In good conditions the animals emerge from their retreats in the morning as the ground warms up and spend all their time searching for food, returning home early only if their stomachs are entirely full. Often temperatures get very hot in the middle of the day and the lizards have to retire to the shade until later in the afternoon. Looking for food accounts for almost all activity at all times of the year except the breeding season. Unfortunately we know nothing at all about the behaviour of savannah monitors during the breeding season.

## How big do savannah monitors get?

We know that in captivity savannah monitors can reach lengths of over 120cm [4 feet], but animals of this size must be very rare in the wild. In the coastal plains of Ghana few savannah monitors ever get larger than 100cm [39 inches] in total length. Cansdale, who lived in the country for many years, never saw one this size[17]. The average size of adults I have caught in Ghana is 33cm [13 inches] body length, 31cm [12 inches] tail and a weight of 753g [26.5 ounces]. The heaviest animal found weighed less than 2kg [4.5 pounds]. Most measurements were taken early in the wet season and I would expect the adult animals to be at least 25% heavier prior to reproduction, but they never reach the weights attained by obese captive specimens. Newly hatched wild savannah monitors are about 13 cm [5 inches] long and weigh 6-7g [0.25 ounces]. This is much smaller than has been reported for hatchlings bred in captivity and probably reflects the greater amount of humidity available to artificially incubated eggs.

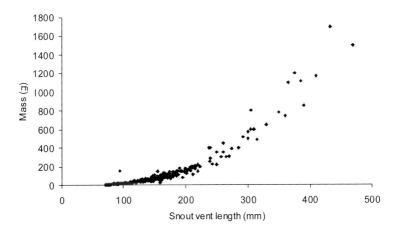

**Figure 21. Size distribution of savannah monitors in the coastal plain of Ghana. [28g=1oz]**

## How fast do savannah monitors grow?

There is no firm data about the growth rates of wild savannah monitors, but we can guess how fast the animals grow over the first six months of life by comparing measurements of hatchlings taken in the first few weeks of life with animals in the same area caught five or six months later. This suggests an average increase

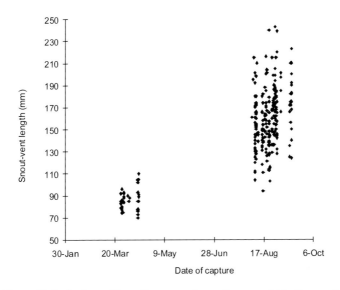

**Figure 22. Body sizes of juvenile savannah monitors caught in the coastal plain of Ghana. [25.4mm = 1 inch]**

from 70mm [2.8 inches] body length and 7g [0.25 ounces] at hatching to 175mm [7 inches] and 100g [3.5 ounces] after six months. There is considerable variation between individuals with some juveniles growing at over twice this rate. The figures are similar to those for the Bengal monitor in northern India and Pakistan[3], with an important difference. Juvenile Bengal monitors accumulate large amounts of fat that sustain them through a subsequent fast of several months. Savannah monitors of the same age do not contain appreciable amounts of fat and so I presume they must continue to feed throughout the first year of life.

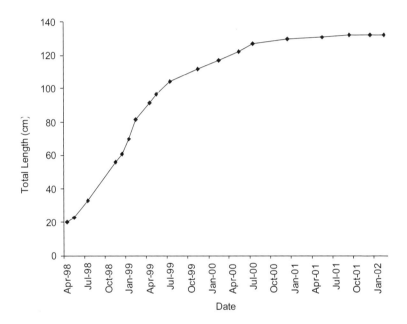

**Figure 23. Growth rate of Rusty, a captive savannah monitor courtesy of Dale Harmon. [25.4cm = 1 foot]**

Data for captive animals indicates that growth rates can be much faster. Dale Harmon's savannah monitor Rusty was 60cm [2 feet] long by the time he was nine months old! He continued to grow rapidly for a further two years, reaching 137cm [54 inches] by the time he was three. Whether wild savannah monitors ever grow this fast or reach this size is unknown.

Figure 24. Rusty as a juvenile courtesy of Dale Harmon

Figure 25. Rusty as an adult courtesy of Mr and Mrs Harmon.

## How do savannah monitors breed?

Unfortunately everything we know about reproduction in wild savannah monitors comes from dead animals[20] or from reports of local animal collectors. So although we know something about the physiology and timing of the reproductive process, we are almost entirely ignorant of the natural history behind it. In both Senegal and Ghana the reproductive organs of both species are inactive for most of the year, begin to grow early in the wet season and produce sex cells towards the end of the wet season, when food has been abundant for many months. Testes and ovaries grow very quickly and peak early in the dry season, when courtship, mating and egg laying take place. The savannah monitor is an extremely fecund animal. Its ovaries are huge, accounting for about 7.5% of overall body weight at the peak of the breeding season.

Female savannah monitor become sexually mature at a total length of about 27cm [10.5 inches] and a weight of 350g –500g [12.5-18 ounces], males probably at a slightly larger size. In Ghana they reach this size in the second or third year of life. In Senegal most breeding occurs around September, in Ghana the season is two or three months later.

The behaviour of reproductive adults remains a mystery, but in Ghana females appear to move out of their usual grassland habitat to lay their eggs in farmland. I suspect that laying eggs around farmland is advantageous because of the abundance of burrows and food for the juveniles, both provided largely by the giant cricket *Brachytrupes*. I also suspect that a great deal of nest making occurs during the hours of darkness, although there is absolutely no evidence for this from free-living animals. Nests we have found have all been in sandy soil, in sunny locations and no more than 30cm [12 inches] deep. The shaft terminates in a small chamber in which the eggs are deposited, the shaft is refilled, sometimes with a plug of vegetation near the egg chamber and almost impossible to detect. When the eggs hatch the youngsters escape by digging directly upwards, resulting in a small round hole at the surface which provides the only clue of the nest's presence. All the nests I have found have shown 100% hatch rate (i.e. no failures). Collectors report that they sometimes find nests full of newly hatched juveniles, apparently waiting for rain before emerging.

In Senegal eggs laid in September hatch the following July[18]. In Ghana the incubation period is usually much shorter, with eggs laid in November and December hatching in March and April. These dates are completely dependent on current weather condition. In April 2001 very little rain had fallen at my study sites, and very few juveniles could be found. A nest that I managed to locate in late April contained eggs that were still some weeks from hatching.

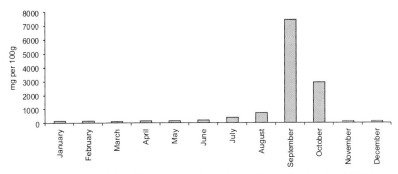

Figure 26. Ovary weight of *Varanus exanthematicus* in Senegal (after Cissé 1976)

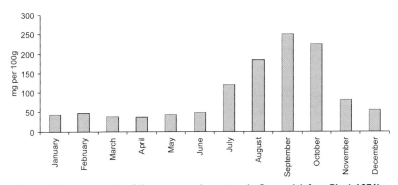

Figure 27. Testes weight of *Varanus exanthematicus* in Senegal (after Cissé 1976)

## How often do savannah monitors breed?

Savannah monitors can be extremely prolific. Clutch sizes are larger than almost all other species of monitor lizard, with 40 or more eggs not being uncommon. We know that in captivity savannah monitor lizards can produce clutches of eggs every few months or even weeks[28], and that a large female could produce over 120 eggs per year. Under natural conditions breeding appears to be restricted to just one or two months per year. It is highly probable that females who have access to sufficient food can produce more than one set of offspring per year, although how often such favourable conditions occur is unknown.

## How do baby savannah monitors live?

When they finally emerge from the nest the siblings all go their separate ways. I have found no evidence that the animals remain together for the first few weeks of life, as has been suggested for some other monitor lizards. However the abundance of resources in farmland mean they do not need to travel far from the nest, and the siblings may remain in the field they were born in for most of the first year of life. At my study sites the juveniles invariably make for the burrows of the giant cricket, *Brachytrupes*. If the burrow contains a cricket the lizard will become an unwelcome tenant, resisting all the insect's attempts to evict it until it becomes large enough to drag the landlord out of the burrow and devour it. Young savannah monitors are voracious feeders and because they have unusually large heads they are able to devour much larger prey than other monitor species of a similar size. Their habitual use of the burrows of giant crickets keeps them out of contact with many of the predators that live in the surrounding grasslands and life seems fairly easy for the youngsters until they eventually outgrow these shelters and have to seek alternative accommodation outside the fields. Very few appear to survive the transition.

## *Are savannah monitors useful?*

Throughout the range of the savannah monitor child mortality is high and life expectancy extraordinarily low. The savannah monitor is extremely important to many millions of people who rely on it as a controller of pests and a source of protein and leather. It is therefore of high economic importance in one of the poorest areas of the world. International trade in the skins of savannah monitor originates mainly from three particularly poverty stricken countries; Chad, Mali and Sudan. Pet trade animals come from the slightly better off countries of Ghana and Togo, but even here it is poorly paid immigrants who collect the animals. Typical profile of a hunter of savannah monitors for skins in Sudan is a subsistence farmer with more than four children and no other work during the dry season. Typical profile for a hunter collecting the animals for the pet trade in Ghana is an illiterate immigrant from a poorer country with at least two children and poor command of the local language. Juvenile lizards are most abundant in the insect-rich fields of farmers who cannot afford pesticides. It seems that throughout Africa it is the very poorest people who have most need of the savannah monitor.

It is perhaps ironic that in places where savannah monitors are collected for skins they are not eaten, whilst in most places they are eaten the skin is cooked along with the meat. During my studies I have often worked with local farmers whose only interest in savannah monitors is as a food item. They usually consider digging the adults out of their retreats as too dangerous, because of the high probability of finding a spitting cobra inside. But they will happily take any lizards they find on the ground or in trees, and are not fussy about the size. On several occasions I have seen families fed a meagre soup consisting of little more than the chopped up bodies of two or three baby savannah monitors.

Figure 28. Savannah monitors provide and important source of protein for
many people in West Africa. Picture courtesy of Nicky Green.

## How many savannah monitors are sold as pets and where do they come from?

International trade in savannah monitors is regulated by CITES, and permits are required from both the source and destination country before the animals can be exported. Whether CITES figures are an accurate guide to the size of the trade is doubtful, because many transactions are simply unreported.

According to CITES figures, between 1990 and 1998 declared imports of live savannah monitors totalled 233,959 animals, whilst declared exports totalled 153,906. Exporting countries were Benin, Ghana, Togo, Mali, Zambia, Burundi, Tanzania, Lesotho, Zimbabwe, Mozambique, Angola and Netherlands. Because only the first four of these countries are home to wild populations of

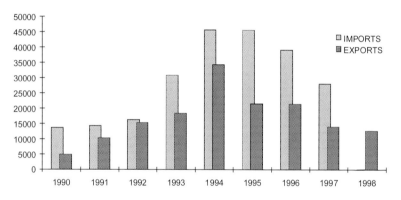

Figure 29. Declared imports and exports of Savannah monitors from West Africa. CITES trade statistics, derived from the WCMC CITES trade database.

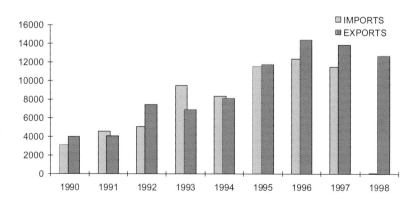

Figure 30. Declared imports and exports of Savannah monitors from Ghana. CITES trade statistics, derived from the WCMC CITES trade database.

Figure 31 (previous page). A young
savannah monitor destined for the
pet trade, Abokobi, Ghana.

Figures 32. *Varanus abigularis*

Figure 33. *Varanus exanthematicus*

Figure 34. *Varanus niloticus* Aswan, Egypt.

Figure 35. *Varanus griseus*, Repetek, Turkmenistan

Figure 36. Savannah monitor can be inquisitive animal when they feel secure.

Figure 37. Two juvenile savannah monitors from separate clutches, bred by Ravi .

Figure 38. Adult savannah monitor from Dawa, Ghana. Note the large ticks in the nostril and ear.

Figure 39. Pair of savannah monitors with female below. Note her shorter, lower and more pointed snout.

**Figure 40.** Savannah monitor from Shai Hills, Ghana. This male probably lost his
tail in an encounter with baboons.

Figures 41. Savannah monitor from Agomeda

Figure 42. Savannah monitor from Kokrobite in the coastal plain of Ghana. Note differences in body colour and substrate.

Figure 43 (next page). Savannah monitor from Bui National Park, Ghana.

savannah monitors the animals from other countries are presumed to be white-throated monitors. Declared imports from these four countries totalled 214,067 animals, with the highest number coming from Ghana (83,357), then Togo (47,809), Benin (19,539) and Mali (2,650). Import and export figures for Ghana are more consistent than for Togo and suggest an overall increase in trade through the decade.

**Fig 44. Searching for animals in an abandoned termite mound is a very dangerous occupation. Any snakes or lizards found will be sold to exporters and eventually end up for sale as pets.**

## Are savannah monitors endangered?

No. The savannah monitor has a very wide range and is very common in many places, including areas where it is harvested in large numbers for the pet trade. Despite a high level of human exploitation populations appear to be healthy wherever the animals' habitat is left at least partly intact. This is a consequence of its ability to survive on hidden invertebrates and its high rate of reproduction. No studies have been conducted to assess populations exploited by the leather trade, but studies of other species (including the closely related Nile monitor) suggest that even where levels of harvesting are high and sustained, populations are still large[16,31].

Intensive collecting of savannah monitors for the pet trade occurs in the Greater Accra region of Ghana. I investigated population sizes in this area and measured the rate at which professional collectors harvest the lizards using a mark-recapture technique[8]. The results indicated a density of 357 juvenile savannah monitors per km$^2$ [0.4 square miles] equivalent to a biomass of 30.9kg [68lbs] per km$^2$, an extremely high density for any vertebrate animal. On average collectors found a lizard every 70-100 minutes and it took them three visits to catch 50% of the animals present.

In the coastal plain of Ghana, where many pet trade savannah monitors originate, the greatest threat to the lizards is the use of pesticides in farmland and the expansion of cities and towns into the countryside. However given the large amount of habitat still surviving and the fact that few farmers can afford pesticides of any sort, the savannah monitor cannot be considered an endangered animal.

## What is Brachytrupes?

*Brachytrupes membranaceus* is a giant (6cm, 6g [2.5inch, 0.2oz]) cricket with an extraordinary life cycle[22]. Males sing at the entrance to their burrows and any approaching females are seized, impregnated and dragged underground to be sealed up in solitary dungeons. *Brachytrupes* is a major crop pest whenever it occurs (often known as the tobacco cricket), but it is of interest to us because of its importance in the life of juvenile savannah monitors in the coastal plain of Ghana. From leaving the nest until they are at least ten months old, the hatchlings are more or less dependent on the crickets for burrows and a substantial part of their diet. *Brachytrupes* crickets are found throughout Africa and western Asia and the relationship is so advantageous to the monitor lizards that it would be surprising if it did not occur in other species. I can only find a single record of a monitor lizard feeding on a *Brachytrupes* species in Asia[3], but am sure that future research will reveal the relationship to be widespread.

Unfortunately *Brachytrupes* is not available commercially. Although some exporters of savannah monitors put them on their price lists there is apparently little demand for them as pets and I am unaware that it is bred in captivity.

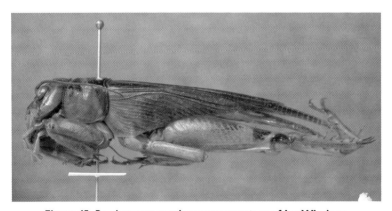

**Figure 45. *Brachytrupes membranaceus* courtesy of Jan Wieringa.**

## Why are savannah monitors so popular?

**Figure 46. Savannah monitors are loved by people everywhere.**

Savannah monitors are one of the most easily available and widely kept large lizards in the pet trade worldwide. There are many reasons for this, some good and some bad.

1. **Savannah monitors are very cheap.** True, but unfortunate because it means that very large numbers of juvenile savannah monitors are being imported each year at ridiculously low costs to importers who can in turn sell them to retailers for a small mark up and still make a substantial profit. The final selling price is still so low that many people buy the animals on impulse before considering the commitment and expense it involves.

2. **Savannah monitors are easy to keep.** In fact savannah monitors are very tough and can withstand months, sometimes years, of abuse and poor conditions. The vast majority of those that survive capture and export are dead within a year, mainly through infestations of internal parasites. Many of the survivors end up as unwanted adults in rescue centres, often available "free to a good home". With the price of newly imported monitors being so low they are viewed as 'disposable' by many, which in turn feeds this vicious cycle. Obviously this type of exploitation cannot continue forever so we must change the way we think of this popular monitor lizard.

3. **Savannah monitors are docile.** Although this tends to be the case with many individuals of this species the key word is 'individual'. Savannah monitors (just like any other lizards) have individual temperaments that span the entire mood spectrum. Most grow accustomed to being handled but it would not be wise to buy a savannah monitor thinking that you will inevitably end up with a lap dog. Some savannah monitors are downright nasty and will not hesitate to bite

a perceived threat. Very docile savannah monitor are more likely to be dying than benevolently placid.

4. **Savannah monitors are ideal for beginners.** Partly true. Certainly savannah monitors are much more suitable for inexperienced keepers than many other species that are commonly available, but the truth is that this is a large lizard with a healthy appetite that may require more care than a first-time keeper is able to provide. Many now tote *Varanus acanthurus* (affectionately known as the "ackie") as the ideal first monitor due to its more manageable size, space requirements and appetite, but also because the available animals are 100% captive bred and therefore free of many of the problems that befall animals taken from their wild environment.

5. **Savannah monitors are fun.** Very true! There is no doubt that the savannah monitor's popularity is also due in no small part to its fascinating appearance and its endearing personality. There are many good reasons for keeping savannah monitors, but it is essential that prospective keepers are equipped with a proper understanding of the commitment they are about to undertake.

**Figure 47. Rusty is an example of a savannah monitor that became part of the family. Courtesy of Dale Harmon**

## Can I buy captive bred savannah monitors?

Hardly ever. Virtually all the savannah monitors offered for sale are taken from the wild. Reports of captive breeding in the savannah monitor are extremely rare, not because they are particularly difficult to breed but because they are usually kept in incorrect conditions. Breeding savannah monitors for profit is not an option because wild animals can be bought from importers for a few dollars, much less than it would cost to raise them in captivity. However some enthusiasts do breed the lizards and wherever captive bred animals are available they should be snapped up. These youngsters are much more likely to thrive and breed than wild caught imports.

## Where do captive hatched, captive born, ranched and farmed animals come from?

Few people, especially animal dealers, seem to understand these terms, presuming that there are farms in Africa where large numbers of lizards are bred for the pet trade. This is completely incorrect. In recent years a large proportion of savannah monitors have been sold as captive hatched, captive born, ranched or farmed. This means that instead of capturing large numbers of juvenile lizards for export, only gravid females are collected. They are kept in captivity until they produce eggs, which are incubated artificially. The females are then "returned to the wild". This gives the impression of being more sustainable and ecologically friendly than dealing in wild caught animals, but in fact the opposite is true for the following reasons.

Adult female monitor lizards are extremely difficult to find outside the breeding season (typically we catch 6 - 10 adult males for every female we encounter). They appear to limit their movements to searching for food and accumulating energy to produce eggs. During the breeding season the females become extremely active as they search for good nesting sites. At this time of year they are easy to collect. The animals are kept in captivity, often in very unsanitary conditions, until they produce eggs, which are then incubated artificially. As soon as they hatch they can be exported as extremely cute babies, not taken from the wild but "captive hatched" from mothers "released into the wild". In fact these animals, now exhausted and stressed, are almost guaranteed to perish. There is little incentive for the "farmer" actually to return them. It would be impractical to take each one back to the place it was caught, and more often than not the lizards are either recycled into the pet trade, sold for meat and skin or just dumped at a roadside. My experiments in Ghana[8] show that about a third of the juvenile population is removed when a group of experienced lizard collectors visit an area, whilst the reproductive population is left undisturbed. Enough youngsters remain to ensure some survivors and so exploitation had minimal impact on the population overall. In contrast when adult females are targeted it is inconceivable that the population would not be affected. Instead of a third of the youngsters being removed, entire clutches are taken and the adult females eliminated permanently.

## How should I keep savannah monitors in captivity?

That's what the rest of this book is about, but the first thing you need to do is forget everything you might have learned in other books about savannah monitors. Other books suggest you keep them like visitors you want to get rid of, but in our opinion you should keep savannah monitors as you would guests in your hotel; offering them as many choices as possible, respecting their privacy and supplying the highest quality food and furniture to ensure their comfort. There is no doubt that keeping them in the manner we suggest is much more time consuming and expensive, but the results are thriving, healthy animals rather than ones that simply die slowly.

## How long do savannah monitors live?

All monitor lizards are capable of living for at least 20 years and 30 years is not unknown. Therefore the savannah monitor has a longer lifespan than many breeds of domestic dogs or cats, a fact that needs to be considered before purchasing one! At present the average life span of a savannah monitor in captivity (discounting those that die before they are sold) is probably less than 12 months. This is due entirely to improper husbandry and is something that we hope this book will help to improve.

## How much space do savannah monitors need?

This will depend on the animals' size – as they grow they will need more space. Keeping young monitors in an enclosure large enough for adults does not work well, so the animals' housing will need to be changed several times as they mature. It is a lot easier to monitor the feeding and progress of babies and juveniles in smaller cages than it would be in a very large cage. Glass aquariums are ideal for juvenile animals but as they get larger it becomes increasingly difficult to find suitably sized (and affordable) glass tanks so what many keepers do at a much lower cost is build their own cage. This can be done with a bit of planning and a small amount of carpentry skill. If you are uncomfortable with building your own cage you can always look around for someone to assist you with this, but remember that an aquarium will be sufficient only for the first two or three months of the animal's life, so some advanced planning is essential.

A group of 2-6 juveniles can be comfortably housed in a 70-90cm [30-36 inch] standard aquarium. A tank 39cm [15 inches] high is much better than one only

**Figure 48. Let your savannah monitors tell you what they need by offering them choices.**

30cm [12 inches] tall because it allows a reasonable depth of substrate and sufficient space to put suitable heat lamps. For adult animals the cage should be as large as you can make it and still be able to provide what the monitor needs. Remember that savannah monitors can grow upwards of four feet long - they will need to be able to move around comfortably! As a minimum we would suggest a cage with dimensions 240 X 120 X 120cm [8 feet long X 4 feet wide by X 4 feet high]. These dimensions will allow ample floor area for walking around as well as allow you to provide a deep substrate bed.

The cage must allow the keeper to provide the monitor with the tools it will need to do its job. The actual size of the cage becomes less important when you think of it in this sense. A well-planned smaller cage can be much better for a monitor than a bigger enclosure that does not provide anything useful. With thoughtful use of furnishings even a moderately sized enclosure can contain a good range of thermal gradients and provide an acceptable home.

## How should I house savannah monitors?

Again, forget everything you might have read in other books about how to keep savannah monitors. Their methods keep them **too cold, too dry and too insecure.** The cage is where the monitor will be living for the rest of its life, therefore it should allow for all life events to take place. A cage needs to hold substrate and humidity, a suitable thermal gradient, provide places for the monitors to hide, search for food and nest. Not to mention, be escape-proof! Savannah monitors will cruise their cages and if there is a weakness in your design they will be sure to find and exploit it. Anything that the animals can destroy will be destroyed and all possible escape routes will be tested extensively.

Physically a cage is simply a box structure that allows you visibility and accessibility to the animals. Important factors to consider when choosing a cage are proper sealing, humidity/ventilation control and the ease with which the lizards can escape. Make sure that the cage will be able to hold the amount of substrate you want to fill it with. Access can be via the top or side, but generally top access is preferred because it is easier or more effective to have a covered top with controlled ventilation to reduce humidity loss. This also provides greater control over escapes when the enclosure is open.

A surprising number of people buy savannah monitors before they have even thought about where they are to live. Although hatchling animals can be kept in glass aquariums at first, they grow so quickly that you may not have time to get larger enclosures finished before they have outgrown their first home.

## Can I buy a cage to keep savannah monitors in?

It is very unlikely that you will be able to find a purpose built vivarium suitable for adult savannah monitors. None of the products available in animal shops are anything near big enough. You are more likely to find a suitable home for the animals at a specialist plastic dealers or a manufacturer of containers. Many people opt to build their own cages, or get more skilled friends or relatives to do the job. Be prepared to make alterations to the enclosure as you learn more about the lizards' needs and preferences.

## What materials can I build an enclosure out of?

When it comes to deciding on a cage for your savannah monitors there is a world of choice. Perhaps the simplest housing is a custom made enclosure such as a galvanised trough or moulded plastic box fitted with an escape-proof lid that allows access and visibility. Otherwise boxes can be built with access via either the top or sides. Most cages made this way will need to be sealed at the joints to prevent moisture seeping into the wood. If you are using a sliding glass type front you will have to make sure the bridge that the glass and sliding track sit on is high enough from the substrate so that the moving parts won't be clogged when the lizards dig and throw substrate around. Some keepers use glass, plexi-glass, or hardware cloth for the accessibility side. Plexiglass tends to scratch and will look unsightly in time whereas hardware cloth allows for a lot of humidity loss and can cause serious rostral damage if the monitor is unhappy with the cage and   is constantly rubbing its nose or frightened and runs into the mesh. Glass eliminates these issues but is more fragile.

Various coated particle boards (such as melamine and MDF) are quick to bubble and warp when the exposed board comes in contact with moisture and can release toxins. They are not recommended. Other materials like plywood and concrete board are more moisture tolerant but even these will need to be sealed to keep out moisture or prevent the release of toxins. Inert waterproof options include polycarbonate, PVC or ABS panels which can be joined together or fixed to a wooden frame. An increasingly popular choice is the use of fibre reinforced polymer (FRP) boards treated with a waterproof resin. These products are available at large home builders' stores.

Building an enclosure is a massive subject with many different solutions. There isn't enough space to cover it in full detail here and we hope it will be the subject of a future publication. The most important things to remember are to make it completely waterproof, escape-proof and deep enough to hold a good bed of substrate. Herpetological societies are an excellent place to get help with your cage designs, which will need modifying according to the advice given in this book. Here you should be able to find someone with experience in cage building or at the very least a contact to someone that can help you out.

## How should I ventilate the enclosure?

An enclosure with a mesh top will lose moisture more quickly than a covered one and this should be kept in mind when you are designing your cage. Ventilating the enclosure requires a balance between allowing air circulation and keeping moisture loss at an acceptable level. Too much ventilation and the enclosure will dry out very quickly, too little and the air will become stuffy and temperatures difficult to control. Some keepers may be able to properly provide humid areas using a screened top while others may find it impossible. The best all-round solution it to use adjustable ventilation situated in the lid of the enclosure where it is easier to enlarge or reduce after a bit of experimentation.

## Can I keep savannah monitors outside?

An indoor cage is recommended to most keepers. Outdoor cages are useful but require a good understanding of monitor behavior to be used successfully. There are many uncontrollable variables that occur outdoors that can present drawbacks to this approach. Before you keep your animals outside seek advice from local reptile keepers. Remember the savannah monitor is a tropical animal and does not endure cold weather in its natural environment. Good information on keeping monitor lizards outside can be found in Robert Faust's excellent book on Nile monitors[23].

49

## What should go on the floor of the enclosure?

Something the animals can dig in. Savannah monitors are diggers, plain and simple. Ravi has raised captive bred babies that were digging amazingly long and deep tunnels at just a few months old. With this in mind keepers must provide their savannah monitors with an appropriate substrate. The bottom of the enclosure should contain a deep bed of material that the lizards can burrow into. You might have read in other books that savannah monitors are best kept on hard surfaces that are easy to keep clean. This is incorrect. You might also have read that letting them live on a natural substrate can cause problems from ingestion of particles, which is also incorrect. Sometimes the monitors will ingest some dirt when they are feeding, but we have seen no ill effects from this and in fact dirt is invariably found in the faeces of wild savannah monitors. Monitor lizards much prefer to live on something that they can dig into. The substrate bed also makes it much easier to maintain proper thermal gradients and adequate levels of humidity. It does make for much more work than a hard flooring, but the benefits to the animals' well-being greatly outweighs the inconvenience to the keeper.

## What substrate should I use and how deep should it be?

Dirt of some kind is ideal. In order to hold a proper burrow the substrate must be of the right consistency, humidity and depth. Being able to go out and dig up your own dirt is nice if this is an option. It goes without saying that the dirt should be free of pollutants and pesticides. Many people have to create their own dirt 'mix' because climate, availability or practicality dictates it. In this case the keeper will have to experiment with different ratios of various substrates to find a suitable one. Sand and soil mixtures are popular, are similar to the substrates the lizards occur on in nature, and have been used successfully to nest savannah monitors in captivity. Getting this ratio right will take a bit of experiment and fine-tuning. In order to maintain sufficient humidity care must be taken not to allow the substrate to dry out. Occasional misting of the dirt should help to prevent this.

Although dirt is not the only substrate that savannah monitors can be kept on it is easily the best. Cypress mulch and aspen shavings can be used but are limited in their ability to hold proper burrows and may hold too much moisture. One substrate to definitely steer clear of is cedar mulch or bark which is toxic to lizards.

If you are able to provide a substrate depth of at least 50cm [1.5 feet] this would be great for the adult lizards. For the majority of savannah keepers this is their first monitor and as such may be overwhelmed by such a need. For many others

**Figure 49. Savannah monitors of all ages love to dig. Keeping them on hard surfaces is not good for their well-being.**

this is simply not possible due to restrictions on space and finances among numerous other reasons. Don't be discouraged however. Savannah monitors will use this depth if you provide it, but it is not essential to have this depth of substrate available to the lizards at all times. The only time it is essential is when females are ready to lay eggs. Females NEED a substrate that is deep enough and deemed usable by her in order to nest properly. At the time of nesting substrate depth cannot be overlooked.

## Should the enclosure have drainage?

Because the substrate will need to be dampened regularly to maintain sufficient humidity, water may build up in the bottom of the enclosure and pose a threat by becoming a breeding ground for fungi and bacteria. To eliminate this risk it's a good idea to build a drainage system that will allow water that seeps through the substrate to escape. This need be no more complicated than the drainage system in a plant pot: a screened hole in the bottom of the enclosure and a layer of gravel under the substrate.

## How often should I change the substrate?

Providing the animals' faeces are removed regularly from the enclosure, the substrate will need to be changed only once or twice per year. So long as it remains smelling "sweet" there is no need to change it. Don't ever use anything to mask the normal smell of the enclosure - monitor lizards are very sensitive and deodorants of any kind will stress them. If the enclosure smells bad enough to need deodorizing it's time to clean it!

## Can I keep my monitor on newspaper?

Please don't! Hard floorings such as newspaper should be avoided whenever possible. They are awkward for the animals to walk on, deprive them of the pleasure of digging and make it difficult to maintain the proper level of humidity in the enclosure. Other substrates to avoid are astroturf and carpeting, in fact any thing that the animals cannot dig up. There is really no substitute for a deep bed of substrate!

## How much heat do savannah monitors need?

The heat requirements of savannah monitors vary from minute to minute, hour to hour, day to day and season to season. How hot they want to be depends on (among other things) the amount of food consumed, the animals' physiological state, the humidity of the environment and their size. So only the individual lizards are able to answer this question. The role of the keeper is to provide the lizards with a complete range of temperature options, and let them decide what is most suitable at any time.

Understanding the importance of proper heating is one of the most important lessons in the care of monitor lizards. We all know that monitors are cold blooded and in captivity rely on their keepers to provide them with what they need to thrive. What has only been realised in the last few years is that monitor lizards require access to much higher temperatures than was previously thought. In recent years monitor husbandry has gone through some changes in thinking. The old way of giving monitor lizards hot spots of 38°C [100°F] was not producing results in the breeding arena. It has been consistently shown that an elevated basking spot plays an important part not just in the captive reproduction of monitor lizards, but in their overall well-being. Ravi keeps his savannah monitors in a cage with hot spots of up to 62.8°C [145°F]! This is much higher than is recommended by other books about savannah monitors, but is a vital aspect of their correct care in captivity.

Of course, whilst depriving the animal of heat will retard its progress, exposing it to too much heat will kill it instantly. Hot spots are provided as an option for the animals; they can take as much heat as they want and then move elsewhere. If the lizards are in cramped conditions it will not be possible to provide hotspots safely and there is a serious risk of the entire enclosure overheating and killing its occupants.

Don't think of lizards getting warm just in terms of basking! Although they like to lie in the sun to gain heat they will also seek out different temperatures in their hiding places. Therefore the range of temperatures below ground need to be as wide as the gradient above ground.

# How should I provide heat?

What you want to achieve is a temperature gradient throughout the enclosure with the coolest areas around 24°C [75°F] and hot spots with surface temperatures up to 63°C [145°F]. This takes very careful planning and experiment. Basically what is required is a basking platform for each animal and a choice of hiding places of different temperatures.

The primary heat source is designed to keep minimum ambient temperature in the enclosure around 24°C [75°F]. In many situations it will be more convenient or economical to keep the entire room close to this temperature. Otherwise, possible sources include ceramic heating bulbs or heat mats/pads on or under the substrate. Because warm air rises it makes more sense to have the heat source at the bottom of the enclosure where it will work more efficiently. However many keepers have reservations about the use of heating mats, because they are prone to overheat, are difficult to check (often the only way to ensure it is working is to touch it) and many models are not particularly effective. Purpose made heat pads might not withstand the attention of large lizards but durable models designed for people can be purchased inexpensively, and larger, almost indestructible models for pigs are available. Choose a model that is adjustable and add a circuit breaker just in case. Depending on ambient conditions and the size of the enclosure more than one primary heat source may be required.

Secondary heat for the hot spots is best provided by way of some sort of lamp - don't use a heat source that doesn't emit light as well. Although there are many types and makes of reptile bulbs that one can buy, among the most easily obtained and cost effective bulbs that provide an excellent source of heat are regular halogen flood bulbs. These can be bought at almost any hardware store and usually at a fraction of the price of brand name reptile bulbs. The hot spot is created by positioning the lamp above a basking surface and adjusting the height until the desired temperature is reached. These hot spots should be big enough for the animal to be able to expose its entire head and body to the heat.

The basking surface should be made of wood (cork bark or planks are ideal) which will absorb plenty of heat and be comfortable for the lizards to lie on. It's a good idea to provide hiding places below and around the basking platform which the lizards can use if they want to get warm but prefer to be in the dark.

As your monitor grows the actual size of the basking spot will have to increase to accommodate the entire body length. This is easily achieved by adding another light (or as many as needed) to the enclosure. A bank of two lights is usually sufficient for an adult savannah monitor. If you are housing more than two monitors in the same cage your bank of lights will probably have to increase to accommodate their needs. Three well-placed halogen bulbs should be able to provide enough coverage for a small group. Another factor to consider when housing a group is that it might be beneficial to provide two basking spots instead of just one. This way the monitors have a choice of where they can bask which can reduce the risk of potential conflict and stress on the lizards.

With all this heat in the cage it is vitally important that the monitor has cool areas it can access to properly thermoregulate. 24°C [75 °F] is a good temperature for the coolest spot in the cage. If you are housing more than one monitor together then it is a good idea to have multiple hide areas where they can escape the heat and each other when they want to. There will be times that the monitors will be together when basking and hiding but there will also be times when they have the need to be apart and your cage setup should allow for this.

## How should I check the temperatures?

Because it is the surface temperature of basking areas that we are interested in, rather than the air above it, the most accurate way to measure the temperature is with an infra-red temperature gun which can be simply pointed at any surface for an accurate reading. A more economical alternative is to use inexpensive maximum/minimum thermometers that have an external metal probe as well as an internal sensor and can be used to measure two parts of the enclosure simultaneously. The probe must be in contact with the basking surface in order to give an accurate reading.

Checking the temperature range in the enclosure will tell you exactly how much heat is available, but the best measure is to watch your lizards' behavior, because that will tell you if the heat available is sufficient, too little or too much. If they spend very long periods under the basking lamp chances are they might like it a little hotter. If they never go near the basking area it is too hot.

## How can I ensure the enclosure never overheats?

By using a thermostat in the coolest parts of the enclosure that will cut power to the heaters when the temperature exceeds about 80°F. Again this will require some experiment and practice.

## What heat sources should I avoid?

Don't ever use heat rocks, which can cause nasty burns. Also avoid anything electrical that looks frayed or damaged, anything that the lizards can destroy, anything that emits fumes and anything that poses a fire risk.

## How much water do savannah monitors need?

Savannah monitors need more humidity in their environment than they are usually given in captivity and will do very poorly in enclosures that are too dry. Over and over again we read in magazines and books that savannah monitor lizards come from very dry areas of Africa and so should be kept in very dry conditions. Completely wrong! The animals are absent from deserts and live in places with seasonal rainfall. Activity is concentrated mainly in the wettest months of the year and the monitors suspend activity when conditions become very dry. Animals in a cage will behave the same way and so it is vital that the enclosure provides them with sufficient humidity to behave normally without having to resort to water-saving strategies. Keeping the lizards on a deep substrate that can be sprayed with water is the best way to overcome this problem. It does not matter if the surface dries out so long as the lower levels are slightly damp. The enclosure should not be steamy but if a piece of orange peel left in the enclosure for 24 hours dries out you can be sure that the lizards have insufficient humidity.

Savannah monitors also require a fresh supply of drinking water at all times. They will drink regularly, but if they soak themselves in the bowl they are telling you that the humidity in the enclosure is too low! Many times the water bowl takes on the added feature of acting as a toilet. This can be convenient since it makes cleaning up easier but the bowl should be thoroughly disinfected and rinsed before putting it back in the cage.

## How often should I spray the enclosure?

This will depend on how humid the air is to begin with, the type of substrate used and the overall temperatures. A light spraying over the substrate every few days or as needed should be sufficient to maintain adequate levels of humidity. The cage should not be damp, but neither should it be bone dry. Most of the time the surface of the substrate should be dry, but the lower levels slightly moist. By spraying one area of the enclosure more heavily you will notice if the lizards take advantage of extra humidity. Problems with skin shedding are often indicative of incorrect humidity.

## What light do savannah monitors need?

This is a topic that generates much discussion and disagreement among the varanid keeping community. Lizards need ultra-violet light to synthesize vitamin D3, and the controversy centres on whether vitamin supplements alone are a sufficient source of the vitamin. The object of this section is not to debate these questions but simply to report what has been successfully used in keeping and reproducing savannah monitors. Ravi has been able to breed savannah monitors successfully without the use of any UV lighting whatsoever. Many other monitor breeders have similar experiences. With this said, it is important to keep in mind that you should dust food items regularly with a high quality vitamin and calcium supplement.

Halogen bulbs by themselves have been successfully used for lighting with many different species including savannah monitors. They provide the essential heat as well as light. Lighting requirements will vary depending on cage size, and personal taste. Many keepers are able to light their cages using the same halogen(s) or spotlight(s) used to heat the cage. This form of lighting has been used in multiple successful breedings of savannah monitors. If your cage is very large then you will probably find that you will need to implement incandescent or fluorescent bulbs specifically for the purpose of lighting.

It is advisable to make sure that all lighting and heating fixtures are securely fastened to the cage so that monitors will not be able to pull them down if they are in reach. Also, if they are in direct reach of the monitor you may want to implement some sort of sturdy mesh screening to prevent burns to the animal or damage to the bulb.

## How long should the lights be on for?

Generally 12-14 hours per day is sufficient, although some of the most successful monitor breeders never turn their lights off! If the lizards have ample places to hide and can choose whether to be in the light or the dark this is not a problem, although obviously 24hr enforced "daytime" would be very cruel. Although there is no evidence that savannah monitors experience a drop in temperatures at night (because they shelter in burrows) some breeders think that a drop in temperature at night is beneficial. The best way to find out what is right for your lizards is to give them all the options and see which they prefer.

**Figure 50. Savannah monitors will never feel secure unless they can hide!**

## Do savannah monitors need to hide?

Absolutely. Security is very important to monitor lizards. Some juvenile monitors tend to be a bit timid at first and will find comfort in being able to hide from any perceived threat. Wild caught sub-adult and adult animals are particularly nervous and will find hide spots a welcome retreat. But in fact all monitor lizards, young or old, tame or not, wild caught or captive bred need to be able to hide at will and still be able to select their preferred temperatures.

There is no one physical definition of a hide spot. Hides can be provided by the keeper or created by the monitor. In either case they are there to serve as a sense of security to the animal. Sometimes one monitor may need to get away from another for whatever reason. Without some sort of retreat that animal could be injured or unduly stressed.

If you can provide a substrate that is deep enough and able to hold a burrow, savannah monitors will dig their own hide area. A burrow will provide shelter and security and is an ideal hide spot. They will generally dig their burrows around the edge of some sort of fixture in the tank or in a corner not out in the open. If you have a plywood platform, split pipes or pieces of wood buried in the ground these can provide some sort of base as the starting point for a burrow. Monitors are smart animals and instinctually know that it is safer to dig a burrow in an area that provides some sort of cover.

It's a good idea to put plenty of hiding places into the enclosure. The lizards may choose to dig their own around them, or they may opt to use those provided from time to time. There are a few things to keep in mind when providing ready-made hiding places. Firstly, monitors like to squeeze into tight spaces where they can feel the sides of the hide around them. Another thing to keep in mind is that hide spots are usually higher in humidity than the surrounding cage and can act as a way for the monitor to conserve moisture. As well as a deep substrate the lizards should be provided with many other hiding places. Hollow logs or cork bark are ideal. Hide spots should be available at both ends of your temperature gradient and in-between as well, giving the animals as much choice of temperatures as they have when they are out and about.

An innovative hide system known as Retes' boards (after Frank Retes – see acknowledgments) has proved extremely popular for many monitor species. The wooden boards are blocked at the corners or on opposite sides so that when they are stacked together a multi-storey block of crevices is created. Stacks can be partially buried in the substrate and set up in such a way that they contain a very wide thermal mosaic that allows the lizards a choice of temperatures without exposing themselves. If the animals need to be captured the stacks can be dismantled and rebuilt very simply. Monitor lizards love hiding amongst

Retes' boards. The size of the blocks determines the height of the hiding crevices and the optimum size for any individual is best determined by giving it a range of crevices to choose from, always ensuring that slightly larger spaces are available for the lizards to utilise as they grow. Larger monitors sometime suffer from some back rubbing after extended periods of sheltering under boards, so if such problems occur use larger blocks or a different type of retreat.

## Should my savannah monitors be able to climb?

Savannah monitors regularly climb trees and bushes in the wild, and will do so in captivity. However it is the ability to dig that is really important for their well being, and so a cage that allows them to climb but provides nowhere to dig is of very little use. Savannah monitors are not graceful climbers and in many cases it will be inconvenient to provide many branches for the animals to climb on because not only will they will fall off from time to time but may be able to reach heat sources and other equipment and sustain injuries as a result. If the enclosure is large enough providing stout branches of any almost any wood (except cedar which is toxic) will greatly increase the temperature options available to the lizards. Ensure that the branches do not allow the lizards to reach cable or lamps and that the enclosure is still 100% escape proof.

## How do I keep the enclosure clean?

Keep the water bowl scrupulously clean. Remove fecal matter from the enclosure as soon as it appears. One massive advantage of using the whole foods we suggest is that feces are much more solid and less messy!

## What should I feed my savannah monitors?

Insects and small rodents are best. In the wild savannah monitors feed on a fairly narrow range of invertebrates, but supplying them with giant millipedes, giant crickets and emperor scorpions would be extremely expensive, so we must use readily available food items to meet our captive monitors' dietary needs. Insects make a great staple food source for hatchlings and juvenile lizards. Crickets are available to almost all keepers throughout the year. They are an excellent food for savannah monitors of all sizes, but they are only as good as the foods they are fed on! All animals destined to be fed to lizards should be kept in the best possible conditions and fed the best and freshest foods available. Crickets raised on a poor quality diet will make inferior food to those raised on a good diet rich in vitamins and minerals, and just before being given to the lizards they should **always be dusted with some high quality vitamin/calcium supplement.** Another group of insects that are becoming increasingly available are roaches. There are a few species that can be purchased or bred by keepers and are quite prolific. Make sure your local by-laws do not prohibit the keeping of these insects. Many adult savannah monitors will chase and eat crickets and other small insects with as much gusto as a hatchling. You should not stop feeding them insects as they get larger, but broaden the diet to include vertebrate prey as well. In captivity mice usually make up much of a savannah monitor's diet. There have been concerns in the past of fur impactions from feeding a rodent-based diet but these concerns seem to be unfounded when digestion is allowed to take its course via a proper basking spot, proper hydration and provision of additional insect food. Some people have access to chicks and are able to feed these young birds to their monitors. These are also acceptable prey items but I (RT) have only used them sparingly. Garden snails are another food source that some keepers have available to them. If you are going to feed snails it is important that they are free of any pesticides. I have had very limited success with snails.

Whether you should feed rodents dead or alive is another personal decision. Monitors are excellent predators and sub-adult to adult savannahs rarely have a problem killing adult mice and small rats. However death by monitor bite is neither instantaneous nor painless and there is always the possibility of the prey animal injuring its predator. Is this a risk you are willing to take? Freshly killed rodents are equally acceptable to savannah monitors. Thoroughly thawed frozen rodents can be used but fresh food is always preferred.

## Do savannah monitors need supplements?

Yes. In the wild monitors get certain minerals and vitamins from their environment rather than directly from food. Vitamin D3 for example is synthesized in

Figure 51. *Iulus* millipedes are a favorite food of adult savannah monitors in the wild, but much too expensive to be considered as food for captive animals. (Photo thanks to Alfred Ojeda)

tissues using ultra violet light and certain minerals may be obtained by rubbing prey into the ground. These options are not available in captivity so it is essential that food is enhanced with a good quality vitamin and mineral supplement. This should be dusted onto insect prey where possible. For savannah monitors that will only feed on mice (there are a few), supplements should be injected into the body of a dead rodent.

## What foods should I never use?

Canned dog food, eggs and strips of meat are not good foods for savannah monitors. Although some people are fans of a turkey-based diet we are unaware of any examples of monitor lizards fed on such a diet that have been able to maintain reproduction for more than about 18 months. These things should be considered last-ditch efforts when no other food is available. Whole, fresh prey items are always best.

## How often should I feed my savannah monitor?

When they are young and growing rapidly it is difficult to overfeed savannah monitors if they have access to proper heat to digest their meals. If the young monitors are digesting their meals properly there is no problem with feeding them as much as they will eat at this size. On the other hand, older animals tend to put on weight more easily and care in feeding may be necessary to avoid obesity. Adult monitors can be fed a few times a week depending on the size of the meals. Only you can judge just how much is enough. Keep track of their digestion and activity patterns to help you make a good decision. Bear in mind that females producing eggs will need large amounts of food whilst adult males are prone to become overweight.

## Can I keep savannah monitors together?

Savannah monitors should be housed together for many reasons. Lone animals are not as much fun to keep as groups and care of a group of animals is not really much more trouble than caring for a single individual. The trick is to get them to do so without any aggressive behavior. If raised together from an early age or if allowed to interact with each other for periods of time, hatchlings and juveniles become familiar with each other and can be kept together with very few incidents of aggression. Even wild caught sub-adult and adult savannah monitors are less prone to intra-specific aggression when housed together as compared to some other varanid species that have reputations for being less than gracious to newcomers, but introducing unacquainted animals is always potentially dangerous.

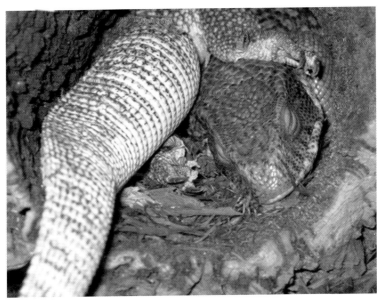

**Figure 52. Savannah monitors will often share hide areas, but it depends on their mood!**

When housing them together remember that you will need to provide sufficient floor space, basking spots, and hide areas for each lizard. Keeping them too cramped can lead to fighting and other problems related to lack of personal space. It has been Ravi's experience that these monitors are best housed in pairs as adults, unless you are able to provide a very large cage space with many hides, basking spots etc. Housing them in pairs gives you better control over keeping track of food intake, and waste materials won't get too out of hand if you miss a cleaning.

Savannah monitors can be very aggressive and eager feeders. Accidental bites are a real risk when feeding more than one animal at a time in the same cage. To avoid unnecessary damage to any of your animals it is advisable to either separate them for feeding or use some other method to ensure they do not fight over the same large prey item. Something as simple as a piece of plywood can be used as a visual barrier to help prevent them from fighting over food.

## How should I choose my savannah monitor?

Ideally you should start with a group of young animals. Older animals will have more difficulty adjusting to captive conditions and it may be difficult to get them to live together peacefully.

When you go to buy your savannah monitor you may be confused with the terms some wholesalers and retailers use to describe the status of the monitors. Some of these terms include CB (captive bred), WC (wild caught), FH (farm hatched) and many themes and variations of these acronyms. In fact unless the animal has been bred locally in captivity it is almost certainly wild caught (see page 45). Buying captive bred lizards should always be considered your first choice because you're sure to be starting with healthy, unstressed animals. Unfortunately at the time of writing, captive bred savannah monitors are not being produced in large numbers so this will probably not be possible. If someone is advertising CB savannah monitors for sale, you as the buyer are within your rights to ask for some sort of proof that they are truly CB, and all honest breeders or dealers should be able to provide you with this. The most incontrovertible proof is a photograph of the animal emerging from its egg!

Whether you buy captive bred or wild monitors, the key thing to look for is alertness. Young savannah monitors are very alert, active and quick to take on a

**Figure 53. Young savannah monitors should be alert and vigorous.**

defensive posture, which includes puffing up, tail whipping and even biting. Look for an animal that is not missing any toes or its tail tip. The monitor's eyes should be open and clear with no watery discharge. It should also have good body weight and a full looking tail. Avoid any animals that look lethargic, have sores or ticks on the body, hipbones protruding or look otherwise unhealthy.

**It is absolutely vital that the animals be tested for intestinal parasites and treated if necessary.** This is because parasites are present in even the youngest wild caught animals, and almost always proliferate to pathological proportions with the unavoidable stress of capture and shipping. Because of the very low cost of savannah monitors many dealers avoid the extra cost of anti-parasitic drugs, with tragic results. Ask the dealers if the animals have been treated and don't be shy to ask for proof. As always, the advice of a competent vet should be sought before diagnosing and treating parasites and diseases.

## Why is my savannah monitor so lazy?

Savannah monitor sometimes have a reputation for being lethargic animals, but in our opinion this "laziness" is a symptom of stress or disease. As we have described earlier, wild savannah monitors are very inactive during dry periods. An enclosure that lacks sufficient humidity replicates these dry season conditions and the animals will respond by keeping activity to a minimum. Secondly, any animal taken from the wild is likely to be very shy, and the lizard may be reluctant to do anything in human company. Providing the animal with enough of the all-important hiding places and giving it time to adjust to its new conditions will probably solve this problem. Thirdly, older savannah monitors do tend to become obese in captivity, refusing to even chase down crickets and not moving for anything less than a mouse. Keeping an eye on the lizard's weight, giving it access to warm enough basking spots and encouraging it to forage actively for insects in its enclosure will spice up its life no end. Finally, and perhaps most crucially, juvenile savannah monitors should never appear lethargic - it's a sure sign that something is wrong.

## How often do savannah monitors shed their skin?

Lizards shed their skin as they grow. Because younger animals grow faster than older ones skin shedding is most frequent in juvenile animals and declines with age. Providing the animals are fed properly and have access to sufficient humidity skin shedding should not pose any problems. Resist the temptation to pull dead skin from the lizards, it will fall off (or the animals will rub it off) when it is ready. It is essential that skin is shed completely, because any patches of dead skin will constrict living tissues leading to more serious problems. Ensure that the lizards have furnishing that they can scratch themselves on and try soaking in water if some stubborn patches of dead skin remain.

## *Do savannah monitors have parasites?*

Under natural conditions savannah monitors are hosts to a wide range of external and internal parasites. These are normally present at low levels and do not appear to be very detrimental to the health of the animals. The stress of capture, handling and shipping allows many internal parasites to proliferate and pose a serious risk (see above). Ticks are bloodsucking parasites that attach themselves to the animals' skin but do not present any major health hazards. Nevertheless they should be removed by dabbing them with alcohol to get them to lessen their grip, and pulling them off with a pair of blunt forceps, ensuring that no jaw parts remain embedded in the lizard.

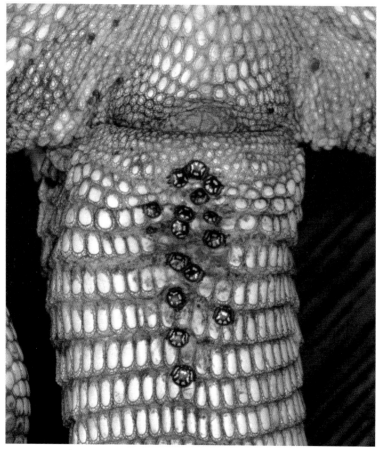

**Figure 54. Tailbase of a wild adult savannah monitor. Tick infestations are unsightly but the real danger comes from internal parasites!**

## What do I do if my savannah monitor gets sick?

Ask a vet! If your lizard was treated for internal parasites when first acquired, and has a good diet (with vitamin and mineral supplements), access to suitable basking temperatures, adequate humidity and plenty of secure hiding places disease should not be a problem. If you suspect your lizard is sick you should seek the advice of a veterinarian, ideally one specialising in reptiles (a local herp society or zoo may be able to recommend one) but any vet will be better able to advise on the correct treatment of a disease than can be offered in a book. Minor injuries (cuts and scratches) should be treated with betadine or a similar iodine based antiseptic. Any signs of infection should be referred to a vet immediately.

Again, the ability to bask at high temperatures appears to be very important in allowing monitor lizards to combat infections and other diseases. Animals maintained in proper conditions rarely succumb to infections and the biggest risk to their health is contact with less healthy individuals. For this reason you should quarantine any new arrivals in a separate room until you are certain that they are in perfect health.

## What do I do if my savannah monitor escapes?

First be very ashamed. Earlier in the book we warned you that if there is any escape route in the enclosure the savannah monitor will find it eventually. If the lizard is loose in the house search all crevices, remembering that the lizards love tight spaces. Under furniture, floorboards, in hollow wall spaces and even beneath furniture upholstery are all possible hiding places, but first you should search in places that are potentially hazardous to the animal; in fires and heaters and behind refrigerators for example. Don't worry if you cannot find it immediately, unless the house is very cold the lizard will eventually come out in search of water and food. Unless it can get out of the house little harm will be done. Leaving shallow dishes of water may tempt it out, but they are unlikely to be tempted out by the smell of food. A dusting of talc on hard floors will provide evidence of the lizard moving about, but there are few safe methods of actually trapping the animals. Very small monitors can sometimes be caught using non-toxic glue boards of the type sold for trapping roaches. The glue is easily removed using vegetable oil. A monitor on the loose outdoors is a more worrying prospect. It is unlikely to travel very far and will most likely take up refuge somewhere in the immediate neighbourhood. Because the lizard is primarily insectivorous when left to its own devices, an escapee savannah monitor does not pose much of a threat to local wildlife. It is at great risk from predation by cats, dogs and vehicles however, and should be tracked down as soon as possible.

65

**Figure 55. An obese savannah monitor**

## *Is my savannah monitor too fat?*

The savannah monitor is a heavily built lizard and healthy adults should be robust but not rotund. Savannah monitors are capable of storing enormous amounts of fat, which is of use in their highly seasonal natural environment. In a cold enclosure, where eating is possible but normal activity and metabolism are not, energy from food is simply stored as fat and as a result obesity is a common problem among captive adults - the result of a combination of insufficient heat or overfeeding. Juveniles don't suffer from these problems but adults can get incredibly fat. Obese animals have problems keeping their bellies off the ground when walking. Severe cases tend be non-reversible and eventually fatal. The most extreme examples have bodies that are as wide as they are long. Prevention is much better than cure for obesity. Feed young animals as much as they will eat but watch the food intake of adults (especially males) as growth slows and don't be afraid to leave them hungry for a few days if they get too fat.

## *What do I do if my savannah monitor won't eat?*

Juvenile animals should almost always be hungry and lethargic individuals who ignore food for days on end are almost certain to die unless they receive veterinary treatment. Adult savannah monitors have a reputation for gluttony and satiated animals are usually hungry again after a very short time. But every now and then the animals may refuse food for reasons that are not apparent. Ensure that reluctance to feed is not due to bullying by cagemates, incorrect temperatures, humidity or some other husbandry factor, otherwise there is no need to get concerned about adult savannah monitors refusing food even for weeks at a time if they appear to be disease-free and in good condition. In starving monitors the bones of the tailbase become visible as the animals loose weight. In healthy animals the tailbase is fat and firm and provides sustenance during periods of fasting.

## Is my savannah monitor growing normally?

Under natural conditions most savannah monitors reach maturity after two or three years. In captivity they can reach maturity in less than a year. How fast the animals grow is not particularly important providing they appear to be healthy and have good appetites. The graphs on pages 25-26 should provide a rough guide to savannah monitor growth, but remember that individuals vary and there are no hard and fast rules about how fast they should grow.

## Are savannah monitors dangerous?

Savannah monitors cannot be classed as dangerous animals, in contrast to many other monitor lizards commonly available in the pet trade. But they are capable of inflicting injuries on people, most usually by scratching. Everybody who handles savannah monitors should be aware that they have very strong jaws. Bites from hatchlings are barely noticeable and quite amusing but adults can inflict severe bites that can become infected. Monitors in general tend to be very reluctant to release a bite once they have crunched down and removing the monitor from your hand or wherever it has bitten you could results in damage to the monitor's jaws if you have to prise them apart. The commonest cause of bites from savannah monitors is hands that smell of food rather than any aggressive action on the part of the lizard. But perhaps the most dangerous thing about savannah monitors is the remote possibility of *Salmonella* infections that have been reported from captive animals. Again this is entirely the result of poor husbandry and an improper diet. We think it is highly unlikely that animals kept in the manner we recommend will ever harbor pathogenic bacteria, but you should always wash your hands with soap and water after handling reptiles.

## Can I tame my savannah monitor?

Savannah monitors are naturally very shy animals and can only be tamed by getting them to respond to you in a subordinate way that probably makes them less likely to engage in breeding behaviour. However many savannah monitors are kept as family pets and in this case it is important that the animals are used to being handled. It is important to state yet again that some individuals never become tame. Having said that there are many tame savannah monitor lizards, apparently leading happy family lives, all over north America and Europe. Providing the lizards feel secure and care is taken when the smell of food is present, it is quite possible to tame savannah monitors providing they are obtained at an early age.

DON'T start off with a tame monitor! That's because the only specimens in the pet shop that have a good chance of survival are the ones that are hissing, striking out with their tails and ready to bite. The ones that tolerate handling (usually passive, sleepy individuals) are sick and probably already doomed. A healthy young savannah monitor will defend itself vigorously against everybody. The trick with taming the lizard is to condition it to not respond to handling as a threat. Start off by leaving the animal alone in its well-equipped enclosure until it feels secure enough to emerge of its own accord in your presence. This may take a few weeks or months but if the animal is being housed properly it will eventually emerge from hiding for long enough to be lifted out without requiring any excavation. Use a pair of thick gloves to begin with, so that the lizard can try biting and (hopefully) learn that it has no effect. The taming process can be greatly speeded up by establishing a routine whereby the lizard is handled at regular intervals, usually around feeding time. Although it is better not to handle the animals much after heavy meals initially it is probably easier to have a satiated lizard to stroke rather than one that is ravenously hungry. Ensure that gloves and hands are kept scrupulously clean of anything that might smell like food. Lizards show a definite preference for where they like to be stroked. In general they are much less tolerant of being stroked on the back than on the head. Monitor lizards probably don't have erogenous zones, but many individuals do seem to enjoy being tickled under the chin or scratched behind the ear. Handle the animal in this way until you feel confident enough to remove the gloves. In time some lizards can become completely at ease, not just with people, but with other family pets. Always wash your hands after you've been in contact with your lizard.

**Figure 56. When savannah monitors get used to people they can be very relaxed. Picture courtesy of Christine Himes.**

## Do savannah monitors breed in captivity?

True captive breeding of savannah monitors is not commonly or consistently achieved. Very few of the hundreds of thousands (perhaps millions) of people who have kept savannah monitors have succeeded in breeding them. We know of less than twenty examples worldwide. The main reason for this is simply ignorance of the animals' requirements. If groups of savannah monitors are kept in the way we have described above there is no reason why they should not reproduce. By raising well nourished and unstressed animals, living in near-optimum conditions, your chances of success are high. The best chance you can give yourself to end up with a compatible pair is to purchase a small group of around 3-4 hatchling or juvenile sized individuals and raise them together. This way they will be familiar with each other and your chances of getting a male and female are higher when working with a group of animals.

## How can I tell the sex of my savannah monitors?

There appears to be no reliable way to  sex very young monitor lizards, but from around five months of age males are easily identified when they evert their hemipenes.  Hemipenes are the name given to the two penises that monitor

**Figure 57. Pair of savannah monitors with female at left. Note her smaller head and less massive snout.**

**Figure 58. Male savannah monitor showing characteristic bulbous snout (see also figure 39).**

lizards are blessed with. The large bulbous decoration at the end of each hemipene is a dead giveaway. Females will also evert, but their hemiclitori are smaller and lack the characteristic decoration at the tips[13]. Eversion often occurs when the animals are defecating. The monitors are still usually very similar in snout to vent length at this time, although in general males grow larger than females. Another indicator that can be used to help in judging sex is behavior. Ravi has noticed that the females tend to be more reclusive than the males. Of course this will only be apparent if your cage allows for the monitors to decide whether or not they want to be seen.

As the monitors reach maturity (this can take less than a year in captivity) it should become easier to determine sexes through an external visual examination. Males tend to be considerably larger than females and the hemipenal bulges are visible at the tail base. Males also have proportionally larger and longer heads than females. Experience counts for a lot when it comes to sexing monitors and savannahs are no exception. It becomes much easier if you have many animals to compare against and whilst identifying better endowed males is rarely a problem, positive identification of females can be more difficult.

By far the best way to ensure you have a compatible pair is to raise a group of juvenile animals together. It doesn't seem to matter how closely related the animals are, because many species have been inbred in captivity over many generations with no apparent problems!

## Is there a breeding season in captivity?

Earlier in the book we talked about the breeding season for savannah monitors in the wild. When it comes to captive breeding there is no one breeding season where they show more interest than another. As long as conditions are conducive to egg laying, it has been proven that they can lay year round. One female in Ravi's collection has multi-clutched by laying as many as four clutches in a year.

## How do savannah monitors mate?

Mating commences in the same way each time. The male approaches the female with small jerky head movements and attempts to mount her. He then begins scratching at the base of her tail with one of his back legs coaxing her to raise her tail so they can copulate. If she is receptive to his courting advances they will proceed to mate on and off over the next few days. Biting is not normally a part of mating and if this happens you should separate the animals and try again later.

## When is the female receptive?

All this mating is triggered by the female cycling. This is the time when eggs have been released from the ovaries and enter the oviducts to be fertilised and shelled. This is the only time that the female will be able to use the male's sperm. A cycling female is not too hard to identify once you've seen it a few times.

**Figure 59. Savannah monitors mating. Picture courtesy of Pier Luigi Vianello.**

Female savannah monitors take on a bloated look for the few days they cycle. If the ova are not fertilized during her cycle they are usually reabsorbed. If the breeding was successful the female will become gravid and the eggs will continue to develop and form shells inside her. This takes place over the course of roughly three weeks. Within this time the female will grow noticeably heavy in the abdominal region, the skin becomes stretched and tight looking. Approaching lay time the female will slowly reduce her feeding and may stop altogether a few days before she drops her eggs - but she should get as much food as she wants!

## Where will the female lay her eggs?

During the approximately three-week period between mating and egg laying the female will become restless and begin digging around her cage looking for a suitable place to excavate a burrow and deposit her eggs. In the days building up to the actual laying you will notice that the female will begin basking more than usual. At this time it is vitally important that you provide areas that are large, deep, moist and private enough for her to dig her burrow in. The author has had success with sandy soil mixtures that are pliable enough to hold a burrow. If the female does not find a suitable spot to lay her eggs in she may hold them which can lead to egg binding and even death. At this point you may need to remove the male from the nesting enclosure because he may harass the female and interfere with her nesting, end up eating the eggs or be attacked mercilessly by the female and severely injured!

The female will dig until she is satisfied with the nest site, then back into the burrow and begin laying the eggs. All Ravi's eggs have been laid at night. The females seem to go into what appears to be a trance-like state when this is happening. Once all the eggs have been laid the female will backfill the hole with her hind legs. During the next few days the she will eat ravenously and should regain her former figure quickly.

**Figure 60. Savannah monitor laying eggs. Spreading eggs on top of the substrate suggests the lack of a suitable nest site. Picture courtesy of Daniel Tupper/ Portsmouth Reptile & Amphibian Society.**

# How do I get the eggs to hatch?

Once the female has finished laying you should carefully dig the burrow up until you reach the eggs. Good eggs will look full and round. Deflated eggs are usually bad and will not hatch. You should be careful not to tumble or shake the eggs when you are transporting them to the incubator. If you happen to accidentally turn them in the first few hours after they are laid it should not cause any harm because the embryo would not be very far developed. If the eggs are turned once the embryo has begun its development they will die.

There are a couple of incubating mediums that are readily available and have a proven track record. Ravi has had good success with vermiculite. Perlite is another incubating medium that has been used with great success with many monitor lizards. The medium should be mixed with water so that it is just damp and not too wet. You want the substrate to be of a consistency so that you can squeeze it and have it just clump together in your fist but with no water dripping from it. If the eggs begin to show dents in the first few days this could mean that the substrate is too dry and may need some more moisture. If you have to add more water be sure not to add it directly to the eggs. The amount of water needed will have to be a judgment call on the keeper's part. The incubation material is put into a plastic box and the eggs half buried in the medium. The box should be covered with just enough ventilation to allow gas exchange but still maintain humidity. The box should be placed in the incubator and maintained at 29°C [84°F]. Healthy, fertile eggs are strong and can withstand a certain amount of error by the keeper.

The incubator itself is basically a box capable of keeping the eggs at the required temperature. It contains a thermostatically controlled heater and sometimes a fan directed towards the bottom of the incubator to ensure an even temperature. Incubators can be purchased or made at home. See Robert Faust's book on Nile monitors for details of how to make one very simply from an old fridge and some bits and pieces[23].

At 29°C [84°F] eggs take approximately five months to hatch. I have seen as much as a two-week gap between the first and last hatchings in the same clutch. Much wider gaps have been reported for other species so this is not uncommon. Do not be tempted to throw the eggs away or cut them open until they show definite signs of death.

As the eggs near their hatch date they become dimpled. Do not add water to your incubating medium at this point or you will drown the unhatched babies. Just wait and with any luck they should hatch all on their own the way they were meant to. Monitor eggs are notoriously difficult to hatch, so do not despair if your initial attempts are a failure. Given a well fed female, an adequate male and a suitable nesting site success is achievable!

Figure 61. Savannah monitor eggs about to hatch.

Figure 62. Newly hatched savannah monitors.

## Can females store sperm?

Maybe – females have been known to store sperm for several months, but there is also increasing evidence that female monitor lizards can sometimes produce viable eggs without any contribution from the male. This terrifying phenomenon is known as parthenogenesis, but thankfully it is not known to occur in humans. How it occurs in monitor lizards, and under what circumstances are still unclear. It is nevertheless a very rare occurrence.

## Does the sex of the juveniles depend on incubation temperature?

No, but what the sex of the juveniles does depend on, or even if juveniles are always born with a predetermined sex are still unanswered questions. There is a great deal about monitor lizards that we know nothing about!

## Anything else you can tell me?

Today there are increasing numbers of people having success with monitor lizards. They all have their own methods and preferences and it would be a mistake to consider what we have said as the final word on the subject. The arts of studying these lizards in nature and getting them to succeed in captivity are still rudimentary and there is a long way to go and much more to learn. The key to success with monitor lizards seems to be giving them what they want, which requires recognising their needs, which can best be accomplished by watching your animals carefully and seeking advice from people who have succeeded in breeding monitor lizards.

We have seen that far from being a lizard that lives in very dry conditions, eats anything and is very easy to keep, the savannah monitor is actually the most specialised of the African monitor lizards and rarely enjoys correct care in captivity. We hope this book will be a step in the right direction.

Probably the most important thing to remember is that the cute baby lizard in the pet shop will grow large and may live for decades. There are many types of lizards much more suited to captivity than the monitor lizards, and as a result there are literally thousands of unwanted adult savannah monitors that somebody once thought would make a good pet. Keeping savannah monitors is a long term commitment, but one that can be extremely rewarding.

Figure 63. Producing beautiful healthy baby savannah monitors is a very rewarding experience.

Figure 64. We still know virtually nothing about the biology and natural history of the savannah monitor. Courtesy of Pier Luigi Vianello.

# Where can I learn more about savannah monitors?

## On Holiday

There can't be a more exciting way to learn about savannah monitors than by visiting Ghana. People call it the friendliest country on Earth and the title is no exaggeration. Rich cultural and natural history, delicious food, extraordinary lack of crime, everybody speaks English and the weather is warm and sunny. I can't recommend it highly enough. Most people expect a holiday in Ghana to be expensive, but because the cost of living is cheap even I can afford it. See the Mampam Conservation website (www.mampam.com) for more details or write to: **The Executive Director, Ghana Tourist Board, P. O. Box 3106, Accra, Ghana.**

## Online

The following websites may be useful:
Daniel's website: www.Mampam.com
Ravi's website: www.TheMonitorSpot.com
Rob Faust's website: www.Varanidinterests.com
Captive bred monitor forum: www.varanus.net
Bernie Eidenmuller's site: www.goannas.net
US Metric Association: http://www.lamar.colostate.edu/~hillger/

## In Print

Numbered literature is cited in the text, the works highlighted in bold are highly recommended.

[1]Anderson, J. 1898. Zoology of Egypt: Volume 1. Reptiles and Batrachia. Bernard Quaritch, London. 371pp.

[2]Auffenberg, W. 1988. Gray's monitor lizard. University of Florida, Gainesville.

[3]**Auffenberg, W. 1994. The Bengal monitor. University Press of Florida, Gainesville. 561pp.**

[4]Auffenberg, W. & I. M. Ipe. 1983. The food and feeding of juvenile Bengal monitors. Journal of the Bombay Natural History Society. 80:119-124.

Bayless, M. K. 1994. Zur Fortpflanzungsbiologie des Steppenwarans (*Varanus exanthematicus*). Salamandra 30(2): 109-118.

⁵Bayless, M.K. & R.G. Sprackland. 2000. The taxonomy of Africa's Savannah and Cape Monitor Lizards. Part I. Reptiles June 8(6):76-85

⁶Bayless, M.K. & R.G. Sprackland. 2000. The taxonomy of Africa's Savannah and Cape Monitor Lizards. Part 2. Reptiles July 8(7):40-47.

**Bennett, D. 1995. A Little Book of Monitor Lizards. Viper Press, Aberdeen. 208pp.**

⁷Bennett, D. 2000a. Preliminary data on the diet of juvenile *Varanus exanthematicus* (Sauria: Varanidae) in the coastal plain of Ghana. Herpetological Journal 10 (2):75-76.

⁸Bennett, D. 2000b. The density and abundance of juvenile Bosc's monitor lizards (*Varanus exanthematicus*) in the coastal plain of Ghana. Amphibia-Reptilia 21:301-306.

⁹Bennett, D. 2000c. Observations on Bosc's monitor lizard (*Varanus exanthematicus*) in the wild. Bull. Chicago. Herp. Soc. 35(8): 177-180.

Bennett, D. 2001. *Varanus exanthematicus*, a very misundertood lizard. Reptilia (GB) 19:43-46.

¹⁰Bennett, D. 2001. Gray's monitor lizard on Polillo Island, Philippines. Reptilia 17:34-38

¹¹Bennett, D. 2002. "Diet of juvenile *Varanus niloticus* (Sauria : Varanidae) on the Black Volta River in Ghana." Journal of Herpelogy 36(1): 116-117.

¹²Bennett, D. & B. Basuglo. 1998. Lacertilia: *Varanus exanthematicus* (Bosc's Monitor): Predation. Herpetological Review. 29 (4) 240-241.

¹³Böhme, W. 1995. Hemiclitoris Discovered - a Fully Differentiated Erectile Structure in Female Monitor Lizards (*Varanus* Spp.) (Reptilia, Varanidae). Journal of Zoological Systematics and Evolutionary Research 33(3): 129-132.

¹⁴Böhme, W. and T. Ziegler. 1997. Grosswarane im Museum Koenig, mit Bemerkungen zu Afrikas grosster Esche. Teir und Museum 5(3):65-74.

[15]Bosc, L. 1792. *Lacerta exanthematica* Act. Soc. Hist. Nat. Paris 1: 25

[16]de-Buffrenil, V., C. Chabanet and J. Castanet. 1994. **Donnees preliminaires sur la taille, la croissance et la longevite du varan du Nil (*Varanus niloticus*) dans la region du lac Tchad. Canadian Journal of Zoology 72(2): 262-273.**

Cansdale, G. S. 1951. Some Gold Coast Lizards. Nigerian Field 16(1):21-24.

[17]Cansdale, G. 1955. Reptiles of West Africa  Penguin Books.

[18]Cissé, M.. 1971. La Diapause chex les Varanides du Senegal. Notes. Africaines. No 131. IFAN Dakar:57-67.

[19]Cissé, M. 1972. L'Alimentaire des Varanides au Senegal. Bull.L'inst. Francais Afr. Noire. ser A. 39:503-515.

Cissé, M. 1973. Evolution de la graisse de reserve et cycle genital chez *Varanus niloticus*. Bull. IFAN t.XXXV, ser A:169-179.

[20]Cissé, M. 1976. Le cycle genital des Varans du Senegal. Bull L'institute Francais Afr. Noire (Sci.Nat.). 38:188-205.

[21]Clos, L.M. 1995. A new species of *Varanus* from the Miocene of Kenya. J. Vertebrate Paleontology 15(2):254-267.

[22]Costa, G., M. Leonardi & A. Petralia. 1987. Reproductive behaviour of the giant cricket *Brachytrupes membranaceus* in the Namib. Madoqua 15 (3): 217-228.

Dunger, G. T. 1967. The lizards and snakes of Nigeria. Part 3. The monitors and a plated lizard. Nigerian Field 32: 170-178

[23]**Faust, R. J. 2001. Nile Monitors. Barrons Educational Series, New York. 95pp.**

[24]Heyden in Ruppell. Atlas Reise N. Afr. Rept. 1: 25.

[25]Horn, H.G. 1985 Salamandra 21(2-3):169-179. Beitrage zum verhalten von Waranen: Die Ritualkampfe von *Varanus komodoensis* Ouwens, 1912, *V.semiremex* Peters, 1869 Sowie die Imponierphasen der Ritualkampfe von *V.timorensis timorensis* (Gray 1831) un *V.t.similis* Mertens, 1958.

[26]Lenz, S. 1995. Zur biologie und Okologie des Nilwarans, *Varanus niloticus* (Linnaeus 1766) in Gambia, Westafrika. Mertensiella . 256p.

Luxmoore,R.,B. Groombridge and S. Broad (Eds.) 1988. Significant trade in wildlife: A review of selected species in CITES appendix II. Volume 2: Reptiles and Invertebrates: 182-207. IUCN. Cambridge, U.K.

Mertens, R. 1942a. Die familie der Warane (Varanidae). II. Allgemeines. Abh. Senck. Nat. Gesel. 465:1-116

[27]Mertens, R. 1942b. Die familie der Warane (Varanidae). III. Taxonomie. Abh. Senck. Nat. Gesel. 466:235-391.

Müller, L. 1905. Der westafrikanische Steppenwaran (*Varanus exanthematicus*). Bl. Aquar. Terrar. Kunde 16: 266-268.

[28]**Retes, F. and D. Bennett. 2001. Multiple generations, multiple clutches, and early maturity in four species of monitor lizards bred in captivity. Herpetological Review. 32(4): 244-245.**

Roder, A. & H.G. Horn. 1994. Uber zwei Nachzuchten des Steppenwarans (*Varanus exanthematicus*). Salamandra 30 (2):97-108.

Rowell, A.J. 1994. Keeping and breeding Bosc's monitor lizard in captivity. Newsletter of the Milton Keynes Herpetological Society. May 1994.

[29]Rjumin, A, V. 1968. The ecology of the desert monitor (*Varanus griseus*) in southern Turkmenistan. Herpetology of Middle Asia. Academy of Sciences, Uzbek SSR. Tashkent.pgs 28-31. [in Russian]

[30]Schmidt, K.P. 1919. Contributions to the herpetology of the Belgium Congo based on the collection of the American Museum Expedition 1909-1915. Bull. Amer. Mus. Nat. Hist. 39:385-624.

[31]**Shine,R. P.S. Harlow, J.S. Keogh and Boeadi. 1996. Commercial harvesting of giant lizards: The biology of water monitors *Varanus salvator* in southern Sumatra. Biological Conservation 77:125-134.**

**Shine, R. Harlow, P. Ambariyanto, Boeadi, Mumpuni, Keogh,J. S. 1988. Monitoring monitors: a biological perspective on the**

commercial harvesting of Indonesian reptiles. Mertensiella 9 (1): 61-68.

Shine, R, Ambariyanto, P.S. Harlow and Mumpuni. 1998. Ecological traits of commercially harvested water monitors, Varanus salvator, in northern Sumatra. Wildlife Research 25, (4): 437-447.

Strimple, P. 1988. The Savannah Monitor Varanus exanthematicus. Part 1. The Forked Tongue 13 (12):8-13.

Strimple, P. 1989. The Savannah Monitor Varanus exanthematicus. Part 2. The Forked Tongue. 14 (1):5-7.

Strimple, P. 1988. The Savannah Monitor Varanus exanthematicus. Part 3. The Forked Tongue. 14 (2):5-8.

Strimple, P. 1988. The Savannah Monitor Varanus exanthematicus. Part 4. The Forked Tongue. 14 (3):7-16.

Switak, K. H. 1998. Living in peril – Africa's Savannah and white-throated monitors. Reptiles. February 1998: 76-89.

[32]Tsellarius, A. Y. and Y. G. Menshikov. 1994. Indirect communication and its role in the formation of social structure in Varanus griseus (Sauria). Russian Journal of Herpetology 1(2): 121-132.

[33]Tsellarius, A.Y and Y. G. Menshikov. 1995. The structure of nesting holes and the protection of clutches by the females of Varanus griseus (Reptilia, Sauria). Zoologicheskii Zhurnal 74(1): 119-128. [in Russian]

[34]Tsellarius, A. Y. and E.Y. Tsellarius. 1997. Behavior of Varanus griseus during encounters with conspecifics. Asiatic Herpetological Research 7:108-130.

Yeboah, S. 1993. Aspects of biology of two sympatric species of monitor lizards Varanus niloticus and Varanus exanthematicus (Reptilia, Sauria) in Ghana. Afr. J. Ecol. 32: 331-333.

# Index

# Other Publications from Viper Press

Viper Press publish works on poorly known and neglected animals and places. All publisher's profits are used to fund conservation work in Africa and Asia.

## A Little Book of Monitor Lizards (1995).
The original edition of this world famous book! Subsequently revised in German language and English editions, it remains the most complete guide to monitor lizards available. 232 pages. 110 colour and 24 black and white photos. 14 drawings, 46 maps, 30 charts. ISBN: 0952663201 **NEW EDITION DUE 2003!**

## The Frogs of Coorg, Karnataka India (1999).
The distribution and abundance of amphibians on a coffee estate in Coorg with details of advertisement calls and larval stages. Covers 21 recognised species and four that are currently undescribed. 139 pages + cassette/CD. 33 black and white drawings. ISBN: 0952663260

## Wildlife of Polillo Island, Philippines (2000).
The tiny island of Polillo off Luzon still harbours an amazing diversity of wildlife. Taxa covered are bats, batflies, frogs, birds, and lizards. Includes a chapter on the rare and endemic fruit eating monitor, *Varanus olivaceus*. 174 pages. ISBN: 0952663252

## Field Guide to the Bats of Madagascar (2000)
Includes details of echolocation calls of virtually every species of bat known from Madagascar and a comprehensive key that works on live animals! 110 pages. Black and white photographs and drawings. ISBN: 0952663287

For full catalogue and to order online see our website at **www.mampam.com**